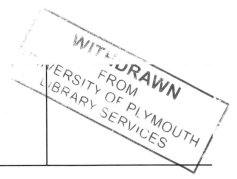

The Reconstruction
of Warriors

The Reconstruction of Warriors

Archibald McIndoe,
the Royal Air Force and the Guinea Pig Club

E.R. Mayhew
Foreword by HRH The Duke of Edinburgh

Greenhill Books, London
Stackpole Books, Pennsylvania

The Reconstruction of Warriors: Archibald McIndoe, the Royal Air Force and the Guinea Pig Club
first published 2004 by Greenhill Books, Lionel Leventhal Limited, Park House, 1 Russell
Gardens, London NW11 9NN
and
Stackpole Books, 5067 Ritter Road, Mechanicsburg, PA 17055, USA

British Library Cataloguing in Publication Data

Mayhew, E. R.
The reconstruction of warriors : Archibald McIndoe, the Royal Air Force and the
Guinea Pig Club
1. McIndoe, Sir Archibald Hector, 1900-1960
2. Guinea Pig Club
3. Surgery, Plastic – Great Britain – History – 20th century
4. World War, 1939-1945 – Medical care – Great Britain
I. Title
940.5'47541

ISBN 1-85367-610-1

Library of Congress Cataloging-in-Publication Data available

Typeset by Servis Filmsetting Ltd, Manchester
Printed and bound by Creative Print and Design (Wales), Ebbw Vale

Contents

Illustrations

Unless otherwise indicated, all cartoons and line drawings are courtesy of *The Guinea Pig* and were drawn by club member Henry Standen, despite his severely burned hands. All photographs have been supplied by members of the Guinea Pig Club and from the archives of the museum at the Queen Victoria Hospital at East Grinstead.

McIndoe joins his patients at the Whitehall
Jack Allaway, Bill Foxley, Claude Allen, Ricky Rix and Winston Churchill
Bill Foxley in the second stage of his pedicle graft
William Foxley's Wedding Day, 28 June 1947
Theatre Sister Dorothy Wagstaff in her office at East Grinstead
Squadron Leader Charles Dutt marries Theatre Sister Dorothy Wagstaff
1952 Reunion pre-dinner group at the Whitehall
Dinner, later that same evening
The 1960 Staff Christmas Party at the Camden Town Marks and Spencer
Bill Foxley, Jimmy Wright and Henry Moore with 'Reclining Figure'
A reunion of the Canadian Guinea Pigs
Spitfire dedicated to the Club by the Battle of Britain Memorial Flight
The Guinea Pig Club Reunion, September 1999
A town's fitting tribute
The boys who came to East Grinstead from all over the world

Text Figures

There can be nothing more terrifying than to be caught by fire without any hope of escape. The whole purpose of armed conflict is to impose casualties on the enemy, but the nature of the wounds suffered varies with the type of service. Soldiers are more likely to suffer from bullets and 'shrapnel'; while sailors, in the days of wooden ships, suffered from the effects of pieces of flying wood. Pilots fight in aircraft driven by engines dependent on inflammable fuel, and a tank-full of the stuff is a deadly hazard.

This book chronicles the consequences of fighting in aircraft and, in particular, the appalling risks to pilots of carrying what amounts to an enormous incendiary bomb in the aircraft with them. It tells the story of the frantic efforts to reduce the vulnerability of fuel tanks. It tells of the equally frantic efforts to find ways to cope with burns and the damage they do to the human body. Above all, it tells of the imaginative efforts to bring the victims back into the mainstream of life.

That is the background to a book about remarkable personalities, about exceptional courage and endurance and about the unstinting support of medical and nursing staff. Dr. Mayhew's history also locates the Guinea Pig Club within the wider history of WorldWar II. It recognises the success of the Club in re-building self-confidence through mutual support, and in ensuring that seriously scarred patients were accepted back into the community. The book is full of heroes and heroic stories, but I think they would all agree that the catalyst for the immense progress in the treatment of burns and in the rehabilitation of the patients was Archibald McIndoe.

Philip

Acknowledgements

It has been my very good fortune to have received the greatest possible help and encouragement during the research and writing of this book from everyone I approached connected with East Grinstead, as well as members of the academic and medical community and many, many others. I hope I have remembered everybody in the list that appears below, and that they are satisfied with the end result of all our efforts.

Jack Toper, editor of *The Guinea Pig*, has been endlessly patient with my questions over three years of research and has provided me with answers, enthusiasm and some wonderful photographs. The Guinea Pig Club's Chief Executive for Welfare, Jack Allaway, has been similarly helpful, especially with the provision of a copy of *New Faces for Old*, in which he starred. From the Guinea Pig Club itself, Betty and John Bubb, Bob Martin, William Foxley and Ronald Humphreyes provided photographs and memories, as did Derek Martin who also gave me access to his remarkable memoirs. Vanora Marland, Sir Archibald McIndoe's daughter, gave generously of her time and encouragement, with the grace and charm that characterises all her work with the Guinea Pig Club and the RAF Benevolent Fund. Two former East Grinstead nurses gave me great insight into their daily lives caring for 'the boys': Nira Hanbury and in particular Rosemary Langford. Nigel Dutt's memories of his parents, who were both on the staff at East Grinstead, were similarly appreciated. I was able to draw on the resources of the Guinea Pig Club museum at East Grinstead courtesy of its curator Bob Marchant. Thanks go to him not only for his efforts on my behalf but also for creating and maintaining this museum from scratch and single-handed, for no other reward than the gratitude of all its thousands of visitors.

This book could not have been written without the support, guidance and imagination of Professor David Edgerton who leads the Centre for the History of Science, Technology and Medicine at Imperial College London. Dr Stephen Bungay, author of *Most Dangerous Enemy*, the best Battle of Britain history to date, was beyond generous in his insights into the tactics and technology of fighter combat, as well as into the mysteries of the publishing process. Dr Matthew Godwin was similarly open-handed with his own research into Civil Defence casualty provision. Professor David French and Dr Paul Addison's close and careful reading of the original thesis also informed the structure of the final manuscript to its great benefit.

Telling the story of Major David Charters and his efforts on behalf of the burned prisoners of war would simply not have been possible without the brilliant detective work of Joan Howe. Through her, I was able to talk to Mrs Margaret Charters, and her children, who provided the photographs and memories of the quiet hero who preferred anonymity when he returned home from Germany. Through the pages of the *Journal of the Royal Society of Ophthalmology* Margaret Hallendorff and her staff enabled me to contact colleagues of Major Charters. Thanks go to Brian Beveridge for details of Major Charters' work post-war, and Archibald Wright Thomson, whose memories of life and medical practice inside the PoW camp system have been invaluable. Two patients of Major Charters in particular provided me with wonderful insights and thanks are due to Jack McEvoy and Lord Hussey for their time and pains. Lord Hussey's autobiography, *Chance Governs All*, is the only other source to mention David Charters and his work at Bad Soden. Thanks go to Dr Hannah Gay for bringing Lord Hussey's autobiography to my attention in the first place.

The medical and technical expertise of Drs Alasdair and Annabel Emslie and Dr Colin Hughes have done much to ensure the accuracy of what follows. Equally appreciated were the comments and encouragement received from Dr Jessica Reinisch and Christian Dinesen. Early and sustained enthusiasm for the project came from Albert Applegath. Peter Mountain's readiness to help with the photographs was gratefully received, as were the sharp-eyed contributions of Tom David and Richard Emslie. Ciaran McConville and the other members of the Debut Theatre

Company were a late but welcome inspiration, as was Karen Kelly who directed the BBC documentary *The Guinea Pig Club*. Thanks are also due to the members of staff from the Imperial War Museum, the Public Records Office, the RAF Museum and the Spitfire Society. As necessary as all of the above was the patience and support of my family, from within whose ranks came the original inspiration for the work.

One final note: in 1942 the East Grinstead Cottage Hospital where Archibald McIndoe ran Ward III changed its name to the Queen Victoria Hospital, which it retains today. For the sake of simplicity, however, the hospital is referred to throughout as 'East Grinstead'.

Introduction

This is a book about how new kinds of warriors and new kinds of heroes were made in Britain between 1939 and 1945. These were the warriors and heroes of the air war who were to be found, not just in fighter formations and bomber streams, but in unexpected places: on long journeys home in wounded aircraft, in battles where the weather was as hazardous as the Luftwaffe and, above all, on operating tables and in hospital wards. The Royal Air Force made these new kinds of warriors and, when hundreds of them underwent terrible ordeals by fire, remade them as very public heroes who symbolised for the Home Front the dangers and exertions of the air war itself.

The Home Front that existed in Britain from 1939 to 1945 was unique. Never in British history had so many ordinary citizens had such direct and prolonged contact with war itself – with action that the vast majority of the population could literally see and hear (and feel if they lived near a bomber station) every day for almost six years. The air war was the war the Home Front knew best, and the sights and sounds of aircraft overhead were daily reminders, just like the ration book and the bomb shelter at the bottom of the garden, of the nation's dangers and exertions. The first significant contact between the air war and the British public was in the Battle of Britain – the first time since the Jacobite rebellions that battle was joined on, or rather, over, British soil. For well over a century British wars had been fought out of sight of the population; even the conflict of 1914–18 could only be experienced second hand by the majority of British citizens (although the German Imperial Air Service mounted several air attacks on London in 1915 and again, sporadically, in 1917 and 1918). Then, for five months in 1940, the population of the south and east of the country watched and listened as the Battle of Britain raged back and forth above their heads and houses. Civilians could see and hear the enemy for themselves, and wait below to see who would prevail. The summer sky was crowded with darting, diving aircraft, their vapour trails, the sound of their engines, and their burning wreckage. The Royal Air Force ultimately held the field and victory was secured in full and immediate public view.

Although the Battle of Britain has come to dominate accounts of the Home Front's relationship with the RAF, its direct impact on the civilian population was local and, like the Blitz which followed, lasted for a relatively short period of time. The Home Front's relationship with the British air offensive, on the other hand, was national and lasted for the entire duration of the war. Indeed, the impact of the RAF on civilian life had begun even before war broke out, with a huge programme of building works to create the infrastructure needed for the planned strategic air offensive. By 1939 there were RAF bases of every description all over the country: as well as Fighter Command stations crowding the southeast corner of England, huge Bomber Command bases dominated East Anglia and other areas; along the western coastline from Scotland to Cornwall stood the squadrons of Coastal Command, patrolling the Atlantic reaches in the campaign against the U-boats; in the Midlands and the Marches were the bustling bases of Training Command, and the air gunnery schools with their aircraft towing target drogues for anti-aircraft gun-crew practice. Close by were the aircraft manufacturers responsible for building and testing new marks of bombers and fighters. Members of the public could even get up close to mighty bomber aircraft when they were put on public display for fund- and morale-raising events such as the 'Wings for Victory' week in 1943. Lancaster aircraft were exhibited in Leeds, Manchester and, of course, Lancaster, as well as in Trafalgar Square in London where crowds for the event were the largest since the Coronation. All air force facilities continually increased in size and activity throughout the war, especially with the arrival of the United States Army Air Force and the movement of huge numbers of aircraft in preparation for D-Day. By 1944 Britain might easily have been characterised as one giant air base.

It was not just the aircraft of the RAF that were such a part of everyday life in wartime Britain; its airmen were also highly visible in British society. Unlike their equivalents in the Army they did not live separately in huge barrack camps, but divided their time between their civilian billets or homes, and their stations. Leave was frequent; bomber crews had one week off in six (more if casualties in their squadron or group were heavy), which was often spent 'in town'. Young airmen, easily identifiable in their blue uniforms with the silver brevet, crowded the trains, nightclubs and theatres of London and other towns and cities, all the time knowing that their war was only a short flight away. It was not just the presence of aircrew amongst civilian society that was markedly different from that of other servicemen, it was also their leaving of it. Soldiers and sailors left on trains to join their units or ships and were away for weeks or months at a time, and it could take equally as long for news to reach family and friends. The absence of airmen was more sudden, and more swiftly and brutally accounted for. Absent aircrew had flown from home soil to engage the enemy in battles that lasted for hours not days. This cycle of presence and sudden absence was repeated, not once a month or twice a year as with the other services, but several times a week, only interrupted by weather conditions, from the outset of the war.

Thus the people of the Home Front knew and understood the air war in some detail. They knew its warriors, their machines, and for the first time in the 20th century they too could see and hear the enemy. And they could also see the price paid for victory, not just in death, but in a new and horrifying form of casualty. From out of the crashed, burning fighters of the Battle of Britain came men whose hands, limbs and, above all, faces had been almost erased by fire. No one could have predicted such injuries, or the airmen's ability to survive them, and accordingly medical provision for severe burns was minimal, and in the hands of one surgeon alone. Archibald McIndoe, civilian consultant surgeon in plastic surgery to the RAF, became responsible for this new form of casualty, and for the men who had suffered it. At a cottage hospital in East Grinstead, under the same skies where the Battle of Britain had been fought, he built an organisation devoted to the care of the burned airman, not just from that battle, but also for the hundreds of burned bomber crewmen who would come after.

McIndoe also fought for his patients in public – and he secured an extraordinary victory on their behalf. Entirely due to his efforts, both the

Royal Air Force and then the public came to recognise and accept not only his patients themselves but also their place and value in wartime society. Rather than hide away these severely disfigured men in the fear that they might compromise the heroic image of the Service, the RAF made them as visible as their uninjured fellows. This was not simply a matter of rewarding casualties from 'The Few' who had defended the homeland so stoutly in the Battle of Britain. Fire was a terrifying feature of the air offensive also, its ever-present danger a threat to the thousands of ordinary crewmen who fought a punishing war night after night over enemy territory. After 1941 the vast majority of severely burned aircrew crawled or leapt from Lancasters, Stirlings, Wellingtons and Halifaxes. It was above all these burned crewmen of Bomber Command who were not only accommodated by the RAF but celebrated, and whose interests were asserted and defended with astonishing vigour. The patients of East Grinstead's Ward III became positive symbols of endurance and, almost unbelievably, of success – their spirit was seen as being as indomitable as that of the Spitfire or of the Home Front itself. And, as the Guinea Pig Club, they became famous throughout the land – the first and only time in modern British history that a large group of casualties achieved a sustained level of public interest and acclaim.

This is a story in which the military efforts made on behalf of injured warriors are given equal consideration with the medical. Not only because of the singular relationship between Archibald McIndoe and the Air Ministry, which ensured an unprecedented level of coherence between the two, but also because of the insights those efforts give us into the world and the war of the Royal Air Force itself. Burn casualties were unique, not just because of the volume and severity of the injuries, but because the environment in which those injuries were inflicted was different from all previous wars and all previous forms of casualty. The RAF was actually involved in the war at two levels: the actual war and a war it had conceptualised long before 1939 and to which, despite practical setbacks and changes of nuance, it remained deeply committed. It was this conceptualised war that determined not only the terms and means of combat but that also reinterpreted the human relationships involved – not only those between the RAF and all its aircrew, but also between the RAF and the public on whose behalf it fought.

The Royal Air Force had thought long and hard about the lessons of the First World War. The world's first independent air service, created in 1918, was the first to conceive itself as a strategic weapon that would revolutionise the means of modern human conflict. Although the parameters of the strategic air concept shifted back and forth throughout the next 30 years, the underlying conviction never wavered: if the RAF assumed the lion's share of responsibility for combat – if fighting power was concentrated in the hands of a relatively small but technically expert force – then the horrors of the previous world war could be avoided. The RAF sought to practise the doctrines preached by the early air theorists Douhet, Mitchell and De Seversky, doctrines in which a strategic air force would have the ability to:

> '... strike at enemy nations <u>as a totality</u> reducing that nation to help-lessness without the time-honoured preliminaries of invasion and mile-by-mile conquest... [providing] the means to disarm an enemy directly, by knocking the weapons out of its hands... through the destruction of its entire war potential.'[1]

The means for knocking the weapons from the enemy were to be bomber aircraft, flown by a technically expert, volunteer force unlike any other seen in previous wars. These were the men who would spare the majority of their fellow citizens from the worst slaughter of the war.

This commitment to the concept of assumed responsibility never wavered. In 1943 a leaflet was distributed by the Ministry of Aircraft Production (MAP) at the factories of Avro which asked the workers to consider the alternative to strategic bombing by the Lancaster aircraft they were building:

> 'What is a Lancaster? ... How long would it take a battery of the heaviest ordnance to reduce 300 acres of an enemy town to pulp? ... Seven men over Germany can do more than a regiment on it... One Lancaster can do more damage in sixty seconds than a battery of heavies in months of blood and sweat... One day we may send men in thousands

with bayonets, guns, cannons, tanks, mortars, shells, scouts, signals, dispatch riders, transport, stores, kitchens and hospitals. That will be to finish the job; to put the final polish on it for good and all. But we are on the job now. We want to save time, labour and precious lives.'[2]

And those convictions held firm long after the war. The memoirs of Arthur Harris, head of Bomber Command 1942–45, described his crews as having, 'the courage of men with long-drawn apprehensions of daily going "over the top".' He had no doubt that, 'the bomber offensive was the only means that I could see, and the results bore out this conclusion, of preventing the Allied armies from suffering enormous casualties when they eventually invaded the continent.'[3]

The RAF was not alone in preparing for future wars, but it was the depth of this conceptualisation that distinguished its plans from other kinds of military preparations. This was an air force 'on a mission' – not just seeking victory but seeking a victory using the specific means at its disposal because only it could spare needless British bloodshed. In the decades before the Second World War, the RAF's commitment to its mission could be seen at all levels of its planning, from the technologies to the tactics of aerial warfare. On the offensive side, bombers became bigger, faster and more heavily armed to outrun or outgun fighter aircraft and deliver ever-increasing payloads. The mirror image of the air offensive was the defence of the British Isles against the same onslaught. Radar was developed to be the eyes of the new fighter squadrons in their defence of the Home Front. Exercise after exercise throughout the 1930s (the last during August 1939) hammered home the message and the mission as waves of bomber squadrons took on Fighter Command to give both sets of aircrew the training they would need to fight the RAF's war. And for those aircrew who would fall during such a war, the RAF developed its own specialised medical service (RAFMS), building 20 hospitals across the country dedicated to the care of its injured personnel, and staffed by leading civilian and military medical specialists.

Despite this intensity of commitment to new concepts, the best-laid plans of the RAF were confounded by the reality of war in 1939. Its aircrew found themselves engaged in aerial combats far more complex than those for which they had been trained. For bomber crews, knocking the weapons out of the enemy's hands was proving considerably more difficult than had been predicted in the air exercises, and fighter pilots found that, rather than engaging hordes of ultra-modern bombers, their war had rather more in common with that of their Royal Flying Corps predecessors, as defence became increasingly a matter of desperate dog-fighting against enemy fighter escorts. Hasty improvisation became the order of the day, as veterans of only months of combat devised tactics that swept away years of pre-war planning. Improvisation was key also to the response of the RAFMS to the savage and entirely unpredictable burns inflicted on the pilots of Fighter Command.

This is the background to the story of the RAF's burned crewmen. It is however far more than a question of simple chronology, as the origins of almost all the elements of the story were intimately connected with the RAF's concept of future air war and its strength of purpose in pursuing that vision. To borrow a metaphor from Arthur Harris, both the seeds of burns injuries and the RAF response to them were sown in the inter-war period, and their reaping began in May 1940 and continues to this day. There was one other element in the story that only partly owed its origins to the RAF's inter-war preparations: the appointment of a civilian consultant in plastic surgery was always part of the medical planning but the fact that the surgeon appointed to the post was the formidable and extraordinary Archibald McIndoe was a matter of pure, enduring luck.

Chapter One

Fire

Although the men of the RAF saw their service transformed in the inter-war years, their two most deadly enemies never changed: the German Air Force and fire, and for obvious reasons this book focuses on the latter. Fire is the most opportunistic of enemies. It can strike an aircraft at any time, not just in combat, but during take-off and landing, or training or routine non-operational flight. In particular military aircraft, where ammunition so often encounters high octane fuel, make easy, combustible prey.

In any aircraft, fighter or bomber, the fuel tank is the most vulnerable component. This vulnerability had been recognised from the outset of air combat in the Great War – even the earliest aircraft had been able to absorb a surprisingly large amount of ammunition, incendiary or otherwise, but it only took one hit on their tanks to finish them. Fuel tanks could threaten an aircraft in two possible ways: their contents could explode on contact with incendiary ammunition, tearing apart whatever section of the aircraft they were housed in, and in all probability destroying the entire machine; or tanks punctured by ammunition, incendiary or otherwise, could leak fuel into the aircraft which could combust if struck by bullets during combat, or simply drain away the pilot's ability to fly back to safety.

One Royal Flying Corps observer wrote of what happened when:

'... the machine to our left was suddenly hit by a shell, full in the main petrol tank! The thing happened so quickly that for a moment I was unable to realise fully what had happened, and remained horror-stricken, watching our companion machine slowly dissolve in the air astern of us.

A second before I had been sitting looking backwards over our tail-plane and regarding what was then evidently a substantial British aeroplane. A fraction of a second later and I saw it hanging in the air before me, its wings floating away from the fuselage whilst a dense black smoke completely obscured the centre section and its occupants. Then, quite slowly, the whole framework twisted sideways, crumpled up, and dived headlong earthwards, wrapped in a sheet of flame.

I sat watching the trail of smoke and fragments which followed it and my companions, down on their two mile journey to the ground and thought many things... it is strange, but at the time I was not so much impressed by the tragic element of the spectacle which I had just witnessed, as by the extraordinary neatness and quickness with which it seemed to have been done. There was something deliberate about it almost suggestive of "legerdemain," and it was only gradually that I realised the significance of that blank space in the formation follow-ing, and the gap at the mess table which would be caused by two stout fellows and comrades of whom fate had robbed us.

I had been actually looking at the machine at the moment of impact, and this, coupled with the fact that the occupants were my friends, left a picture in my memory which I do not often care to revive.'[1]

RFC pilots were only too well aware of the dangers of fire, nicknam-ing petrol 'infernal liquid', 'the hell brew' and 'orange death'.[2] Britain's leading air ace in the Great War, Edward 'Mick' Mannock, was obsessed with this form of death, describing to new recruits to his squadron the horrors of 'flamers' and how he would shoot himself rather than endure the grisly fate he had arranged for at least six enemy pilots during one month alone in early 1918.[3] On hearing of the death of his main rival in the German Imperial Air Service, Manfred von Richthofen, he was heard to say that he hoped the Red Baron had, 'roasted all the way down'.[4] One of Mannock's fellow aces, James McCudden, met just such an end, trapped in his aircraft, but leading American ace Major Raoul Lufbery preferred to take his chances with gravity. After failing to put out a fire by switch-ing off his engine and sideslipping his aircraft (whilst balanced on the head faring so he could keep hold of the joystick), Lufbery finally gave up and leapt from his burning Nieuport aiming hopelessly for a small stream 200 feet beneath him. Horrified onlookers saw his body slam into the ground.[5]

Pilots continued to dread the effects of fire on both themselves and their aircraft. In 1935 students of the RAF Staff College composed essays on how they saw the future of the air services. The winning entry described how a pilot at 'Cranwell 1985 AD' was, 'injected yesterday with a heavy dose of anti-crash asbestos mixture and… had not quite got over the effects yet.'[6] Back in the real world, Sholto Douglas, who commanded 43 and 84 Squadrons in France in the First World War and was later Deputy Chief of the Air Staff, recalled in his memoirs how terrifying the threat of fire was to all airmen:

'On one patrol early in 1917 I was flying formation with my squadron when we were suddenly attacked by some Huns. After the first flurry was over I glanced across at the next aircraft beside me in our formation and I saw that the observer, poor devil, was standing up in the back seat agitatedly trying to call the attention of his pilot to a glint of flame that was just starting to appear along the side of their aircraft. A moment later there was a violent explosion and the whole aircraft disintegrated.

Such a sight was all too common in our flying of those days, and so far as I was concerned it was one of the most horrible that one could witness.'[7]

By 1916 efforts were under way in both the British and French air services to try and reduce such 'all too common' horrors. The search for a solution was based on the principle of wrapping the tank in some sort of elasticated material, such as rubber, that would slow incendiary bullets down sufficiently so they would not ignite the contents of the tank. The material would be constituted in such a way so that it could be expected to swell and stretch on impact so as to close or seal any ruptures and prevent leakage, as well as absorb the shock wave caused by the effect of ammunition striking the unit. This system of 'self-sealing' fuel tanks became the model for all subsequent investigations into aircraft fuel safety by both Allied and German air services and remains the model today. (As a result of the destruction of Concorde AFR 4590 on 25 July 2000, tanks of the remaining Concorde fleet were given extra self-sealing layers of Kevlar to avoid the danger of their combustion by flying debris.)[8]

In July 1917 the first trials of 'non-leaking petrol tanks' were made at the behest of the French Air Service. They had been invented by a Belgian Army engineer, Lanser, and were constructed from a double-hulled metal casing which sandwiched a patented fibrised rubber compound. They had proved successful when the French fired Brock incendiary ammunition at them and had been passed on to the British to undertake similar tests.[9]

The British Air Board tested two of these 'Lanser' tanks the following April but they did not perform to RFC or Admiralty satisfaction. Despite this British reluctance, by 1918 the Lanser tank was standard in the majority of French aeroplanes, and some had even found their way into RFC aircraft, action undertaken unilaterally by British squadron commanders in France (just as some British airmen took to equipping themselves with parachutes in the late summer of 1918, spurred on by the offer of a 20 per cent discount on their life insurance from Lloyds of London if they did so).[10]

Dissatisfaction with the performance of the Lanser gave a tremendous momentum to Britain's own tank protection research, and further momentum was given by the realisation of the possible application of satisfactory measures in airships. Soon Orfordness, the joint forces experimental research station in Suffolk, overflowed with engineers from the Army and Navy blasting away at tanks wrapped in petrol-resisting cloth, tanks with fireproof covers and non-metallic petrol tanks made of plywood and chemically treated fabric. By 1918 all this effort resulted in a tank evolved from the Lanser model with three layers of felt, three of India rubber, soft soap between each, and a cage of iron gauze to resist expansion shock. Known as the M.I.D. pattern, this tank became standard issue in all two-seater aeroplanes (except trainers) from 1918.[11]

Research into tank safety did not end with the war. The newly independent RAF took over responsibility for a variety of investigations into the problem, and moved the entire programme from Orfordness to the former aircraft factory that had become the Royal Aircraft Establishment (RAE) at Farnborough. Here the relationship between tank safety measures and aircraft design became complicated, as RAF technologies – especially fighter technologies – evolved to meet the very specific strategic demands of a newly-conceptualised air war.

By the mid-1930s it was recognised that the bomber would not necessarily always get through, and that with a combination of ground-based early warning systems and efficient fighter aircraft, deployment of a viable defensive system was possible. This meant that fighters had returned to the heart of British strategic thinking, but in an entirely different form from their predecessors of the Royal Flying Corps. Rather than engage other fighters, the intention of fighter tactics was now to catch and kill large self-defending formations of bomber aircraft. To do this they had to be extremely fast and capable of steep and rapid ascent, as well as carrying the maximum weight possible of armament in order to break up formations of bombers. In contrast to the more gradual evolution of bomber aircraft design, fighter design in the 1930s was completely transformed as wood and fabric biplanes became sleek metal monoplane fighters, the Spitfire and Hurricane.

Much has been written about how the shape of the new fighters determined their speed, but it was just as much about the contents of their fuel tanks. And it was not simply a matter of the switch to high octane fuel, but also of the relationship between the fuel tank contents, the fuel tank locations and the shape of the aircraft. The new fighters were single engined, which gave the requisite acceleration and speed, but they also required one large single fuel storage space in the fuselage. Their compact fuselage shape, part of the aerodynamic styling integral to the speed of the new monoplane fighters, meant that no extra weight could be accommodated at the rear or base of the fuselage. Speed also required that the undercarriage retract inside the airframe during flight, which resulted in the wheels being stored during flight in wing wheel wells. Guns were also mounted in the wings, further reducing the space for fuel storage inside these components. (In the end the Hurricane had half its tank allocation in the wings, but the Spitfire had none.) Wings also played a part in determining the location of the engine parts. Wing chord and span in relation to the fuselage height demanded a heavy front load, especially the Spitfire's elliptical wing design. This was satisfied by placing the main fuel tanks for both aeroplanes behind the engine in front of the cockpit and pilot. In the case of the Spitfire (before 1942) *all* the liquid storage was directly in front of the pilot: 48 gallons of high octane fuel in the upper tank, 37 in the lower tank, 5.8 gallons of oil and 15 gallons of glycol coolant. In the case of the Hurricane, the reserve (or gravity) fuel tank of 28 gallons, an oil tank of 7 gallons and the glycol tank of 18 gallons were between cockpit and engine, with a main fuel tank of 25 gallons in each wing.

The fuel itself was key in securing greater speed and lift. Previously using the 87 octane version, both fighters were given a sudden and dramatic power boost by switching their Merlin engines over to high octane fuel early in 1940. The change to a 'rich mixture response' 100 octane fuel significantly increased climb rates and engine efficiency. A second innovation was the introduction of constant speed propellers which, in conjunction with the high performance of 100 octane, allowed aircraft to achieve top take-off rates of 3,000 rpm from the moment they left the ground.

In May 1938 Brian Shenstone, chief engineer at Supermarine, made an ostensibly friendly visit to the Messerschmitt aircraft manufacturing works to observe the speed trials of the German aircraft. Although he was not allowed in the factory, he met with Willi Messerschmitt and observed the latest marks of the Messerschmitt 109 and 110 both in flight and on the ground. On returning to Britain, Shenstone went hotfoot to the Air Ministry to report his findings. He told them that Messerschmitt was just as concerned with speed and wing shape as they were at Hawker and Supermarine, but with rather better success, particularly on the speed front. His recommendations regarding the speed trials of the Hurricane and Spitfire were accepted by the technical department of the Air Ministry, who noted:

'It seems clear [from Shenstone's report] that is is inadvisable to proceed with a record attempt with the Spitfire. [It has been] suspected for some time that Germany was waiting for us to do so in order to do a better one immediately afterwards.'[12]

Shenstone's report to the Air Ministry also demonstrated how thorough was the understanding of the RAF's offensive capabilities and ambitions throughout British aviation. He helpfully noted that:

'The B.F.W. [Messerschmitt] factory comprises seven units scattered around the aerodrome, each part complete in itself, including the canteen, so that dislocation due to a direct bomb hit would be a minimum. A guess at the number of workers employed is 5000 to 6000.'[13]

Efforts of men like Shenstone at Supermarine meant that the designs of the new fighters were able to meet all the demands of the RAF strategists, but in doing so they also created a new set of problems for the tank safety specialists of the RAE. Nevertheless, despite slow progress in designing sealant systems in the 1920s, by 1936 a full range of tank protection systems had been developed. The principle was the same as that of the Lanser tank model in which the existing metal tank was covered with chemically treated rubber linings. Three different versions of this model were produced which varied the thicknesses of both the metal and rubber components so that by 1938 all British aircraft, regardless of size, model or purpose, could have their petrol tanks sealed, and their crew's safety made more secure.

There was a very significant 'but'. Part of the RAE's testing criteria for the three successful sealant systems was their effect on each aircraft's performance. For the bombers the sealant systems added as much as 100 pounds to the overall weight of the aircraft but had no measurable effect on their performance. This was not the case for the fighters. Early in 1939 the RAE forwarded its report on tank protection to the Air Ministry, with an appendix that reported the results of tests on fighter sealant systems. The results were incontrovertible and highly problematic.

Aircraft	Added Weight of Sealant System	Reduction in Capacity	Reduction in Maximum Range
Spitfire	40lb	11 gallons	17%
Hurricane	30lb	11 gallons	19%[14]

Reducing the performance of the new fighters by up to one fifth, and therefore compromising their ability to pursue enemy bombers, was never going to be acceptable to the RAF. In November 1939 a meeting was called with the Director of Operational Research (DOR) in the chair which made clear the position on the strategy/safety calculus that the RAE had presented.[15]

'FIGHTERS/SPITFIRE

... if full self-sealing tankage was provided in the Spitfire the loss in fuel would amount to 11 gallons, which was 17% of the total fuel capacity. D.O.R. said that this was a very serious reduction, as the fuel supply at present was no more than adequate. After some discussion it was suggested that an attempt should be made to fireproof the tanks in the same fashion as those of the Messerschmitt. RAE were now investigating this method. It was agreed that there was no acceptable alternative to this. D.O.R. mentioned that the Spitfire was well armoured in front, and its speed made it comparatively immune to attack from astern.

HURRICANE AND DEFIANT

The provision of self-sealing tanks on these aircraft would involve similar large reductions of fuel capacity. It was agreed that they should be dealt with in the same way as the Spitfire.'[16]

The meeting had opened with a firm statement of the RAF's commitment to the principle of providing 'self-sealing protection for 100 per cent of the fuel tanks' of its aircraft. In practice this meant that 100 per cent of the bomber fleet departing for the defence of France would eventually have full sets of sealed fuel pipes and tanks but that the squadrons of the new fighters which went with them would not.

The decision ultimately to prioritise strategy over safety was reiterated at the highest levels. In December 1939 Wilfrid Freeman (Air Member for Development and Production) responded to a number of enquiries from serving RAF officers about fuel tanks.[17] In a memo *Protected Tanks – Summary of Action in Hand*, Freeman was frank about the priorities for fighters:

'New Types

Fighters are, generally speaking, not easy to deal with, as space for fuel tanks is restricted...

Hurricane, Spitfire, Defiant – Present Position:

New tanks of reduced capacity would be required. Air Staff cannot agree to reduction of fuel on these types. Solution is being sought to devise a thin cover, which would render the tanks fireproof.'[18]

The RAF's decision regarding the safety of fighters was not as cold-blooded as it might seem at first glance. Not only were RAF leaders firmly convinced that just such a 'solution' to the tank issue would be found by the RAE, but it was thought that fighter design and fighter tactics would mitigate the risk until then. Freeman's memo reminded his audience that pilots were protected 'against the return fire of bombers by their engines, and by bulletproof glass and armour for their heads and chest respectively'.[19] Furthermore the RAF believed that the form and the tactics of combat in which the fighters would be engaged minimised the risk. They would be attacking self-defending bomber formations from the rear, using their superior rates of speed and climb to assemble into fixed positions behind the bombers. Each fighter would make its attack and then peel away beneath its target, therefore remaining out of range of the German armament for most of the engagement. Not only would these tactics protect them but it was also thought that the invading aircraft suffered from a technological flaw. Hugh Dowding, head of Fighter Command in the Battle of Britain, noted:

'... at this time the return fire from German bombers was negligible. They had concentrated on performance as [the] principal means of evasion... and the four guns which they carried... were practically useless. Our own fighters... were virtually immune to the fire of unescorted bombers.'[20]

But the Royal Aircraft Establishment's engineers and scientists at Farnborough did not allow themselves the luxury of such optimism, and their search for suitable tank protection systems became increasingly desperate as war began to deliver its first aircraft casualties. It was not only the British casualties that caught their attention but also the German ones; from October 1939 any intact enemy aircraft engines and fuel tanks were delivered with due haste to Farnborough for comparison with their British counterparts. In November they got the petrol tank from a Heinkel 111A that had been forced down in the Lammermuir hills.[21] Tests with 0.303-inch incendiary ammunition (the standard RAF calibre) fired through a sheet of 204 duralumin (a main alloy of aluminium with low density and higher strength to weight ratios) to simulate the aircraft exterior proved that the Germans had a safety system at least as effective as the British version. Bits of a Dornier salvaged from the sea off Wick found their way to Farnborough, as did those from a Junkers 88 which had crashed on the Northumberland coast. An Arado seaplane's collapsible floating tanks made for an interesting study, as did the Semape-like coverings of an Italian Savoia Marchetti S.82. Indeed, so urgent was the priority for fuel tank safety that Farnborough even gained access to the relevant British intelligence. One such report came from a Dutch rubber manufacturer, Koolhaven, where a Captain von Gijen recommended their flexible tanks for use in Dutch aircraft. Unfortunately his recommendation was made slightly less than two weeks before the German *Blitzkrieg* overran Holland, and a month before the plant was destroyed by British bombers attacking the aerodrome next door.[22] When Farnborough finally got its hands on the nearest equivalent to the British fighters, the Messerschmitt 109, it was found to be of no help to their investigations, and indeed they noted the far worse dangers posed to German pilots by their fuel tanks:

'... the tank had no self sealing covering. The tank was roughly in the form of a letter "L". It was fitted in the fuselage directly behind the pilot's seat but separated from the cockpit by a bulkhead, the foot of the "L" passing under the seat... [bullet] holes would have emptied the tank in a very short time.'[23]

So, whilst the RAE searched desperately for the means to secure their greater safety (made worse by increasing shortages of natural rubber), pilots of Spitfires and Hurricanes were to rely upon their tried and tested tactics for countering predicted enemy attacks at the minimum risk to themselves and their aircraft. But the reality of the Battle of France was that it set a pattern that was to be repeated in the Battle of Britain: pilots

DON'T OPEN YOUR HOOD TILL THE LAST MINUTE.

Even the RAF's own handbook took a somewhat optimistic view of the dangers posed to their pilots by fire

found themselves engaging the enemy in ways that had far more to do with their Royal Flying Corps predecessors than with the many exercises in which they had practised 'modern' air tactics. Bombers did not come in large self-defending formations but with fighter escorts, and fighter squadrons came hunting for other fighter squadrons as part of the overall assault.

The pilots of the RAF found themselves in combat that was complex and chaotic as aircraft used ever higher speeds, and where attacks could come from any angle. Being shot at from all sides meant there was a far greater chance of incendiary ammunition striking the very large fuel reserves at the front of the British fighters. Once again, French skies were full of aircraft fighting, crashing and burning. British fighters were shot down in such alarmingly high numbers, and with so little advantage being gained, that finally the rump was brought home in an effort to preserve some form of defensive force for what was now seen to be the inevitable assault on Britain.

The defence of Britain followed hard on the heels of the fall of France, so quickly, in fact, that there was hardly any time for reflection on the lessons of continental defeat. Wherever possible veterans of the fighting were rushed into training units to impart their experience of the real, rather than conceptualised war in the air. But above all there was no time to understand that there were new human costs to be paid for the war in the air; that realisation would come from the Battle of Britain itself.

There was one one further element of the environment of the inter-war period which had as significant a bearing on the RAF casualty-by-fire as any of the above. What follows is a brief explanation of the medical solution to the problem of wound shock. It may seem worlds away from the bomber and the fighter squadrons but when seen in combination with the strategic and technological background, it is a key component. Put simply, up until the end of the 1930s severe injuries, especially severe burns, killed nearly everyone who suffered them almost immediately. After 1939 they did not. Suddenly there were patients where before there had only been corpses, and those patients often required a complex, exceptional and long-term response to their condition from the relevant medical specialists.

Little has been written about this most fundamental of medical break-throughs, perhaps because the process lacks the drama and instant success stories of developments such as penicillin treatment or vaccination. Instead, throughout the 1930s a series of low-level, incremental improvements were made, not in well-funded laboratories or high-profile teaching hospitals, but in emergency rooms and ordinary hospitals where doctors slowly but surely pushed back the limits of existing clinical understanding of the processes involved in the human body's initial reaction – shock – to its severe wounding.

For the burn victim, shock takes a particularly virulent form. The body loses catastrophically high amounts of liquid at the site of the burn, and goes into secondary shock as the rest of the system attempts to compensate for this loss by shifting fluid around the various organs of the body in an attempt to keep each one viable. One by one kidneys, liver and finally the brain are compromised by the loss of liquids and proteins and within 24 hours the patient literally dies of dehydration and starvation. Failure to understand and compensate for this fluid shift meant that, to take a typical example, in the Glasgow Royal Infirmary burns ward in 1937, half of the serious burns patients were dead in 24 hours and three-quarters within three days. And if patients managed by some twist of fate to survive burn shock, they were then almost certainly done for by infection. The reality for burn casualties in the inter-war period was that seriously injured patients were given a little saline, a large dose of morphine and then taken home to die. Without adequate means to address the systemic catastrophe caused by a serious burn, it was no wonder that the burned patient was always regarded as terminal, and furthermore, 'in the early years the over-30% burn was rarely admitted to a teaching hospital, for the case was virtually hopeless and certainly a danger to others.'[24]

In the 1920s doctors had begun giving shocked patients small transfusions of saline in an attempt to counteract fluid shift, but fears about side effects meant it was never given in sufficient amounts to make any real difference. More often than not the result was simply to prolong the inevitable by a couple of days, but an important precedent – of transfusion therapy being used to treat fluid shift – had been established.

The 1930s saw the most significant breakthroughs in the treatment of burn shock as doctors began to explore the full range of uses of plasma (the universally compatible liquid medium that transports blood and proteins through the body). Saline and plasma were combined to produce a new range of transfusion therapies that could not only replace the lost fluid in the system, but also the proteins that are lost with it. Once again, an important precedent was set, but this time clinicians did not hold back in their efforts to understand the full potential of such therapies. Transfusions were given in increasingly high amounts, several times a day, and with their effects closely and carefully monitored by nursing staff:

'... staff developed a complex system of calculations that matched the size and depth of the wound trauma site with the fluid shift it would generate and the requisite amount of transfused plasma and saline.'[25]

Fewer and fewer patients died of their injuries and by the outbreak of war this most significant of clinical breakthroughs had, almost imperceptibly but just in time, become an accepted part of emergency medicine.

If confirmation was needed that modern medicine had found the solution to secondary wound shock, no-one would have had to look any further than the RAF hospitals in the summer of 1940. Here lay men, first a few from the Battle of France, and then in greater numbers from the Battle of Britain, who should have died from their injuries but did not. What had at first seemed a straightforward strategy/safety calculus for the RAF in regard to its fighters had become complicated not only by the realities of combat but also by contemporary medical developments. These developments presented the RAF and its medical service with living, human consequences of decisions made in the inter-war period. For the RAF this was an immediate emergency, not only for the valuable pilots suffering the injury, but for the service itself in compensating for their loss, correcting its causes and caring for the air war's unforeseen human consequences.

Chapter Two

The Burning Blue

In the summer of 1940, the RAF found itself Britain's last line of defence against the seemingly unstoppable onslaught of Nazi Germany in Western Europe. The line held, but the RAF's new kind of war fought with new kinds of fighters exacted a new kind of price for victory, as several times a week for the entire duration of the Battle of Britain members of its aircrew turned up in hospitals all over the south of England with up to one third of their body tissue, including face and hands, burned away. The very worst injuries occurred as follows:

8 August	J.W.C. Squier	64 Squadron	Spitfire
12 August	A.G. Page	56 Squadron	Hurricane
14 August	J.A. Anderson	253 Squadron	Hurricane
16 August	R. Carnal	111 Squadron	Hurricane
24 August	K.B.L. Debenham	151 Squadron	Hurricane
26 August	R. Lane	43 Squadron	Hurricane
31 August	T.P. Gleave	253 Squadron	Hurricane
31 August	M.H. Moundsen	56 Squadron	Hurricane
1 September	B.R. Noble	79 Squadron	Hurricane
3 September	D.W. Hunt	257 Squadron	Hurricane
3 September	R.H. Hillary	603 Squadron	Spitfire
6 September	Z. Krasnodebski	303 Squadron	Hurricane
7 September	J. Koukall	310 Squadron	Hurricane
11 September	W. Towers-Perkins	238 Squadron	Hurricane
15 September	R.H. Holland	92 Squadron	Hurricane

15 September	C.A.L. Hurry	46 Squadron	Hurricane
17 September	R.D. Dunscombe	312 Squadron	Hurricane
23 September	D.J. Aslin	257 Squadron	Hurricane
24 September	H. Bird-Wilson	17 Squadron	Hurricane
1 October	G.H. Bennions	41 Squadron	Spitfire
5 October	J.W. McLaughlin	238 Squadron	Hurricane
15 October	A.J. Banham	229 Squadron	Hurricane
17 November	E.S. Lock	41 Squadron	Spitfire
28 November	P.H.V. Wells	249 Squadron	Hurricane
Date of injury unknown:			
	R.D.F. Day	141 Squadron	Defiant
	J. Lowe	236 Squadron	Hurricane
	J.F. Macphail	603 Squadron	Spitfire[1]

Later, some of those pilots told of their experiences in their burning fighters, some in published memoirs, some in the pages of *The Guinea Pig* magazine. Early in the battle Geoffrey Page was hit by bullets from a Dornier bomber when he was separated from the rest of his formation:

'Surprise quickly changed to fear, and as the instinct of self-preservation began to take over, the gas tank behind the engine blew up, and my cockpit became an inferno. Fear became blind terror, then agonised horror as the bare skin of my hands gripping the throttle and control column shrivelled up like burnt parchment under the intensity of the blast furnace temperature. Screaming at the top of my voice, I threw my head back to keep it away from the searing flames. Instinctively the tortured right hand groped for the release pin securing the restraining Sutton [safety] harness.'

Page finally escaped from his Hurricane with his parachute intact and descended towards the sea:

'It was then that I noticed the smell. The odour of my burnt flesh was so loathsome that I wanted to vomit. But there was too much to attend to. The coastline at Margate was just discernible six to ten miles away. Ten thousand feet below me lay the deserted sea... I began to laugh. The force of the exploding gas tank had blown every vestige of clothing off my thighs downwards, including one shoe.'

Page hit the water but the injuries to his hands made it almost impossible to get free of his parachute:

'The battle with the metal disc [the parachute harness release mechanism] had to be won or else the water-logged parachute would drag me down to a watery grave. Spluttering with mouthfuls of salt water I struggled grimly... pieces of flesh flaked off and blood poured from the raw tissues.'

Eventually Page got himself free of the parachute but his injured hands betrayed him and he was unable to grip his hipflask which sank below the waves. Page was eventually rescued by a British merchant ship but the pain of his immersion should not be underestimated:

'... acute misery passed by as the salt dried about my face injuries and the contracting strap of the flying helmet cut into the raw surface of my chin. Buckle and leather had welded into one solid mass, preventing removal of the headgear.'

On his arrival at the RAF's main hospital at Halton, Page was treated for his wounds and:

'Not wishing to see the needle enter the skin, I looked away and upwards, catching sight of myself in the reflector mirrors of the overhanging light. My last conscious memory was of seeing the hideous mass of swollen burnt flesh that had once been a face.'[2]

Roy Lane was hit in the engine by a Messerschmitt 109 whilst attacking a formation of Heinkels over Portsmouth. His oxygen supply was hit, causing him to pass out but:

'As I fainted I saw a dim red glow in front of my eyes – but I didn't understand what this was until I came to at a lower altitude. I found that my Hurricane was not only on fire but was diving – upside down. Luckily I was hanging by my straps which enabled me to keep my face out of the flames a good deal. Even so I was unable to open my eyes, due to the intense heat... the rolling motion of the aeroplane blowing the flames still hotter.'

Lane eventually got clear of his aircraft, probably as a result of the straps burning through, allowing him to fall out of the cockpit, but he ended up with his parachute attached to his boots. To remedy this, he tried to remove his gloves and helmet:

'The helmet and left hand glove came off all right but my right hand glove was burned and shrivelled on to my hand which had been in the flames most of the time. I managed finally to get that glove off but unfortunately a lot of skin came off with it, leaving my hand very raw indeed.'

Lane managed to land whilst still upside down where he was found by a corporal who asked if he were hurt. In his article for *The Guinea Pig* Lane commented that:

'... the question seem to me, in view of the fact that I was limping badly, my hand was cooked, my face was red with burns and my right trouser leg was burned off – superfluous to say the least.'[3]

Tom Gleave was part of a two-squadron wing attacking a formation of Junkers 88 bombers when he was hit by incendiary ammunition:

'I was about to pull up to attack... when I heard a metallic click above the roar of my engine. It seemed to come from the starboard wing and I glanced in that direction, but a sudden burst of heat struck my face, and I looked down into the cockpit. A long spout of flame was issuing from the hollow starboard wing root, curling up along the port side of the cockpit and then across my right shoulder... I had some crazy notion that if I rocked the aircraft and skidded, losing a bit of speed, the fire might go out. Not a bit of it; the flames increased until the cockpit was like the centre of a blow-lamp nozzle. There was nothing to do but bale out... The skin was already rising off my right wrist and hand, and my left hand was starting to blister, the glove being already partially burnt off. My shoes and slacks must have been burning at this time but I cannot remember any great pain.

I undid my harness and tried to raise myself, but found I had not the strength. I was comforted by the thought that I had my gun ready loaded if things came to the worst.'

Gleave eventually decided to roll out of the open cockpit cover:

'There was a blinding flash, I seemed to be travelling through yards of flame; then I found myself turning over and over in the air but with no sense of falling.'

On landing Gleave inspected his injuries:

'With an effort I stood up and surveyed the damage. My shoes still looked like shoes and I found I could walk; why I don't know, as my ankle and each side of my right foot were burnt and my left foot was scorched and had several small burns. My slacks had disappeared except for portions that had been covered by the parachute harness. The skin on my right leg, from the top of the thigh to just above the ankle, had lifted and draped my leg like outsize plus-fours. My left leg was in a similar condition except that the left thigh was only scorched, thanks to the flames having been directed to my right side. Above each ankle had a bracelet of unburnt skin: my socks, which were always wrinkled, had refused to burn properly and must have just smouldered... My Service gloves were almost burnt off, and the skin from my wrists and hands hung down like paper bags. The under side of my right arm and elbow were burnt and so were my face and neck. I could see all right, although it felt like looking through slits in a mass of swollen skin, and I came to the conclusion that the services of a doctor were necessary.'[4]

Maurice Moundsen was part of a standing patrol when he was hit in an attack on a bomber formation over Colchester:

'Cannon shells smashed into the left side of my Hurricane and I received a lot of shrapnel splinters in my thigh and leg before the same 109, or possibly another, hit the gravity tank and I was instantly in an inferno. I was sitting in the blast from a blow lamp, so I scrambled out just as fast as I could... I landed by parachute at Great Dunmow where I saw the skin on my hands hanging off in what appeared to be shreds of tissue paper...'[5]

The most famous pilot memoir of all, Richard Hillary's work *The Last Enemy*, opens with this description of his injury:

'I felt a terrific explosion which knocked the control stick from my hand, and the whole machine quivered like a stricken animal. In a second, the cockpit was a mass of flames; instinctively, I reached up to open the hood. It would not move... I remember a second of sharp agony, remember thinking "so this is it!" and putting both hands to my eyes. Then I passed out.'

Hillary regained consciousness outside the aeroplane and landed in the water where his life jacket kept him afloat:

'I looked at my watch: it was not there. Then for the first time I noticed how burnt my hands were: down to the wrist, the skin was dead white and hung in shreds: I felt faintly sick from the smell of burnt flesh.'[6]

Zdzislaw Krasnodebski, of the famed Polish 303 Squadron, remembered how 6 September 1940 was a black day not only for him, but also for the squadron when seven out of the twelve aircraft that departed for combat failed to return:

'Guided by radio we were to attack a bomber formation flying toward London at the height of approximately 20,000 feet. I was approaching one of the enemy bombers – it was plainly in my sights and I started firing when at that moment I sighted the shattering glass falling out from my instrument panel. I noticed brightly burning gasoline pouring out of the severely bullet-damaged cockpit and filling it with flames.'

Concerned that, once falling under his parachute, he might become an easy target for German fighters, Krasnodebski delayed jumping from his increasingly dangerous aircraft. When he deemed it safe enough to jump, smoke in the cockpit made it almost impossible to find the hood release handle. Finally he located it and jumped. His descent was so rapid that it extinguished the flames on his clothing but, 'It was then that I became conscious of the agonising pain in my badly burned hands and legs.' The Polish airman also faced another danger peculiar to his nationality:

'As I was descending there appeared another hazard; the soldiers of the Home Guard emerged from the surrounding bushes and moved in my direction with their rifles ready to shoot, apparently they suspected that I might be one of the German parachutists... This difficult situation was not likely to be helped by the sight of the unfamiliar Polish uniform I was wearing – nor by my scant knowledge of the English language. Possibly, only the inborn English self-control and "sang froid" saved me from unexpected consequences.'[7]

South African Pat Wells was injured during the so-called 'forgotten months' (November and December) of the Battle. On 28 November he became Adolf Galland's 56th kill when the German ace attacked his Hurricane. Wells was shadowing a group of Messerschmitt 109s when:

'The next thing I knew was an attack from below, I took evasive action and howled on the R/T but nobody heard or saw this lethal attack. I was only able to take a little more evasive action before my controls were shot away and the well-known "Hurricane Fire" started.'

Wells struggled to exit the aircraft but first one foot then the other became trapped under the instrument panel: 'I made two unsuccessful attempts to get out but was finally thrown out.' As he did, part of the Hurricane's tail hit him, dislocating his shoulder and leaving him effectively with only one hand with which to find the ripcord. Luckily (and untypically) Wells was partly protected:

'Gloves saved my hands from the fire... With skin hanging down in sheets from face and legs I was taken to Leeds Castle Emergency Hospital (the smell familiar to Guinea Pigs of grilled pork was in my nostrils for weeks afterwards!).'[8]

These pilots' accounts of their injuries demonstrate much of the typical RAF flair for understatement. However, when read alongside an eloquent and vivid modern account of burning, some appreciation of the reality of this type of casualty can be gained:

'Being on fire is unforgettable. You will recall those seconds with crystal clarity for the rest of your life. In fact, those who don't remember usually don't survive: fire strikes so fast that if you are knocked unconscious, you stand very little chance. The human body can tolerate only a few seconds in the intense heat and airlessness of a hot fire...

Speed of reaction to a fire or scald is absolutely vital to survival. And yet the experience of surprise actually disables you. So stunned are you to find yourself in the flames that you are literally immobilised. There is a momentary inability to do anything – and in those seconds the damage can be done… Words can hardly describe being on fire: painless, breath-taking, all-embracing, hot, life-threatening, "Help!" Thinking is not really coherent in the instant of inferno. You know instinctively that your life is in the balance. For a split second you think of loved ones. There are voices and screams. The heat is totally enveloping and stifling. Air is desperately short – rather like being breathless under water.

To escape the flames is to feel total release from hell. Fresh air is gasped in. Many fires today are compounded by clouds of noxious fumes, and clean air is all the more gratifying… You are certainly oblivious to the damage you have suffered… [because] the extent of pain is dependent upon how severe your burns are: the deeper they are, the less painful they will be, because the heat will destroy the nerve endings in your skin… [but] for all your facial wounds you are still remarkably sane, emotional and, above all, alive.'[9]

All of the above pilot-casualties had their injuries inflicted upon them by the same combination of circumstances. Seated immediately behind their main or gravity fuel tanks they took the full force of their fuel exploding in their faces (and many had wing tanks explode on them as well). So similar were both the causes and pathologies of their injuries, in fact, that they were given their own medical name, 'Airman's Burn'. The burn was characterised by deep, whole thickness burns to areas of great functional importance, primarily the face and hands. Whole thickness burns are the most serious of all, where all skin tissue is destroyed, including sebaceous glands, hair follicles, sweat glands and nerve endings. An RAFMS memorandum later defined the injury:

'This is a burn of almost unvarying characteristics due to the sudden exposure of unprotected parts of the body to intense, dry heat or flame, as though the entire patient were thrust into a furnace for a few seconds and withdrawn. The distribution is characteristic:-

(i) Both wrists and hands, particularly the backs, the fingers, often the entire surface of the hands. If gloves have been worn, only the wrists are involved. Holes in glove fingers have been responsible for severe localised burns...

(ii) The face in the "helmet area". When goggles are pushed back, the forehead, eyebrows and eyelids may be severely burned. Usually, the eyelids near the lash edges escape. The eyes themselves are not often burned. The oxygen mask may protect the face but the cheeks, nose and ears are often involved.

(iii) The neck between the chin and collar, extending on both sides to the mastoid area [temporal bone behind the ear].

(iv) The anterior and inner surfaces of the thighs if the trousers are thin. The lower legs between the trousers and boot tops if flying boots are not properly adjusted...

Deep, searing burns, usually of "third degree", involve areas of tremendous functional importance – the hands and eyelids in particular.'[10]

The airman's burn pathology also included, 'contact burns where hot material, usually portions of the plane, directly touch[ed] a trapped or unconscious person in a crashed machine.'[11]

The bizarre confluence of military and medical factors that combined to create this new and unpredicted patient group also created problems for the RAF in terms of the less severe burns inflicted on its aircrew. In 1939 41 RAF aircrew suffered burns serious enough to merit sustained medical attention, paperwork, and above all, removal from duty. In 1940 there were 378 men in that category (and that figure is probably on the low side as casualty reporting was a low priority on bases in the thick of the fighting). Their burn injuries break down are shown on the table overleaf.

There were, therefore, nearly 400 men of the RAF rendered incapable of active duty by burn injuries during 1940, the vast majority of whom were pilots of Fighter Command. At first glance the figure seems negligible in the context of a world war, but it was all too important when seen against the specific background of the Battle of Britain. These men were removed from the front line at a time when, according to the man in

Burn Injuries to RAF Aircrew During 1939–40[12]

Location of Burn	Number in 1940	Number in 1939
Head	2	5
Face/mouth	77	7
Eye/lids	14	4
Ears	14	—
Neck	2	1
Chest	3	—
Back	2	2
Abdomen	2	—
Buttocks/pelvis	2	—
Lower arm+hand	97	6
Upper arm	23	1
Shin+ankle+foot	91	12
Upper Leg	49	3
Total burn injuries Home Force	378	41

charge, Hugh Dowding, 'the heavy aircraft wastage… ceased to be the primary danger, its place being taken by the difficulty of producing trained fighter pilots in adequate numbers.'[13] Fighter Command literally needed every man it could get, particularly during, 'the dour campaign of attrition in August', when the tide of the battle appeared to be running against it.[14] The nature of burn injuries made these the worst possible wounds a pilot could suffer, as the treatment for even relatively minor burns could remove an airman from his squadron for several weeks or months – a short period in general medical terms, but in the specific situation of August/September 1940, a whole battle's worth. Dowding commented on this specific problem in his Despatch:

'As regards our casualties, we generally issued statements to the effect that we lost "x" aircraft from which "y" pilots were saved. This did not of course mean that "y" pilots were ready immediately to continue the Battle. Many of them were suffering from wounds, burns or other injuries which precluded their return to flying temporarily or permanently.'[15]

German tactics, as well as the scale of their daily attacks, were stretching British human resources to their limits. 'Free chase over England' was the order posted daily on the notice board of Adolf Galland's squadron stationed in France.[16] German fighters and bombers could strike at the south-east of England from a long line of bases that stretched along the Channel coast from Cherbourg to Antwerp. Fighter Command had to revert to the concept of standing patrols where 12-aircraft squadrons could average 45–60 flying hours in just one day. Such standing patrols, disliked in the inter-war period for their 'uneconomic' use of manpower, placed a further strain on a system that was increasingly reliant on trainees being put prematurely in the front line.

Decisions made the previous year about fuel tanks ensured fighter response was kept at its optimum – Spitfires and Hurricanes kept pace or outflew the German fighters, despite the RAF pilots' lack of training for 'free chase' RFC-style combat. But the human cost was high, and, for want of pilots, the battle was almost lost. Unsurprisingly the situation gave a desperate momentum to the ongoing process of finding tank protection systems suitable for fighters. Late in 1939 the RAE had begun testing a material known as Linatex with a view to installing it in fighters and reported it to be 'very promising'. A Blenheim fitted with a full set of Linatex-sealed pipes and tanks was fitted out and sent for service in France, returning for testing in 1940 to the satisfaction of all concerned.

The RAE described Linatex thus:

'Linatex is the trade name for a special form of rubber which is manufactured in British Malaya from fresh rubber latex using a patented process which is claimed to preserve and impart valuable qualities in a degree peculiar to the material. It is produced and stocked in the form of sheets of various thicknesses. Strong joints can be made by a simple cold cementing process and it can, also, be bonded to other materials. The rubber is unusually tough and resilient and has great resistance to abrasion and penetration. It swells when exposed to the action of petrol or oil but does not dissolve. It is claimed to be almost non-ageing and to be less affected by cold than most other rubber products.'[17]

Approval was given for initial installations to production line fighter aircraft in May 1940 and as a result a supplement was issued to the RAF Mechanics Manual on *Protected Fuel Tanks for Aircraft*.[18] The actual installation process turned out to be slow and patchy. Stocks of the rubber needed to manufacture Linatex had to be assembled. The manufacturer, Wilkinson Rubber, undertook to train Hawker and Supermarine contractors in the fitting and installation of the Linatex system, but this was a far more complex process than installing the three older systems used on bombers:

'Linatex is composed of four layers of rubber sheeting and cotton duck [which] are fitted to the tank and are attached by means of special solutions, the cover being finally doped [treated with chemicals] to shrink it, and hold the rubber layers in close contact with the tank shell... Whilst the patching processes are relatively simple, the tank covering operation [the tanks were dressed in close-fitting, layered rubber jackets] entails a large amount of cutting, fitting and sewing layers of material to fit tanks of varying shapes and sizes, therefore only such competent personnel as fabric workers should undertake the complete covering operations. Strict cleanliness should be observed in the handling of the materials and precautions should be taken against them making contact with dust, oil, grease or any foreign matter that could prevent adhesion between the layers.'[19]

And there was a war on. Bases where the modifications to service aircraft would be made were on high alert, men and machines were constantly being moved around the country to make up for losses, and RAF priorities lay in the precarious day-to-day operations, not in fulfilling complicated aircraft retro-fit instructions. Dowding's Battle of Britain Despatch highlighted another constraint on installation efficiency:

'So far as our Fighters were concerned, the wing tanks in the Hurricane were removed and covered with a fabric known as Linatex which had fairly good self-sealing characteristics. The reserve tank in the fuselage was left uncovered as it was difficult of access, and it was thought that it would be substantially protected by the armour which had been fitted. During the Battle, however, a great number of Hurricanes were set on fire by incendiary bullets or cannon shells, and their pilots were badly burned by a sheet of flame which filled the cockpit before they could escape by parachute.'[20]

Although there were a number of factors that aggravated pilot burn injuries (pilots often discarded goggles and gloves that would otherwise have protected their hands and eyes, and their clothing was often impregnated with oil from assisting ground crew with rapid aircraft turn-arounds), the Dowding Despatch alludes to the possibility that certain aspects of fighter design itself may have made the problem of fire worse. Losses to burn injuries were disproportionately high among the pilots of Hurricanes, even allowing for the higher proportion of Hurricanes to Spitfires flying in the battle. Whilst it is impossible to determine whether or not pilots of Spitfires were more likely to suffer fatal injuries, there is good evidence that the Hurricane posed more of a danger of serious non-fatal injury to its pilots than its stablemate. Two among the 'great number' of Hurricane pilots who fell victim to this design problem described what could happen:

'Flight Lt. Nicholson… was leading a section surprised by an Me.110. The aircraft had self-sealing wing but not gravity tanks. It was hit by cannon shells one of which hit and set fire to the gravity tank. He attacked the Me.110 and shot it down. He could not see the flames but 'flakes' of paint came from the tank. The dashboard also crumbled with the heat – some of it dropped on and burned his legs. By this time the aircraft was at 15,000 feet in a vertical dive doing 400mph. He managed to get both feet on to the seat and jump clear after opening the hood. He did not disconnect either his R/T or oxygen. This pilot did a delayed drop which he thinks put out the flames from his trousers… '

Flight Officer Zatonski had a similar experience when he:

'… was flying a Hurricane without any self-sealing tanks. He was shot down by a Mc.109 and his aircraft caught fire in the gravity tank. The flames were colourless; he knew he was burning by the heat and by the flakes which came back from his tank.'

Flying Officer Sutton was another who fell victim to a design fault peculiar to the Hurricane which increased the pilot's chances of serious burn injuries. The area in which the wing met the body of the aircraft (the wing root) was not closed by any armour plating or sealing mecha-nism, creating a direct channel from fuel tank to cockpit that pushed exploding petrol directly towards the pilot most efficiently. Flying Officer Sutton was:

'... flying alone and had exhausted his gravity tank when he was attacked from the port beam. His port wing tank was hit and set on fire. He had the hood half open and yellow flames came into the cockpit from the wing tank via the wing root end which is not sealed off from the fuselage.'[21]

Burn injury figures appear to back up theories about the dangers of the unsecured wing root. The 1940 figures show high incidences of burns to those parts of the pilot's body nearest the wing root (lower arm and hand, 97; upper arm, 23; shin, ankle, foot, 91; leg, 49). Word appears to have got around amongst Hurricane pilots about the increased risk from their aircraft. Pat Wells' awareness of 'the well known "Hurricane Fire"' has already been noted, and Wing Commander Tom Neil commented in more detail on, 'the fire problem in Hurricanes', during the Battle of Britain itself after a member of his squadron had been badly burned:

'A known fact was that the fire in a Hurricane caused by blazing fuel presented the pilot with a desperate and fearful crisis. In a matter of two or three seconds, the aircraft became untenable and the act of opening the cockpit hood for the purpose of baling out, had the effect of drawing the flames into the pilot's face. There were lurid tales of dashboards melting and running like treacle and the more imaginative of us found heartless amusement visualising scenes in which all the instruments dropped like stones into the bottom of the cockpit.

At first it was thought that the reserve fuel tank, located in front of the dashboard and containing about 30 gallons, was the source of most such fires but it soon became obvious that this was not so. The two wing tanks were the main culprits. Not only were they easier to hit and puncture – the reserve tank was largely shielded by the engine, the pilot and armour plate – but there being no blanking planes between wings and fuselage, the blazing fuel was drawn into the cockpit by the natural draught pattern, particularly if the guns had been fired and the linen patches which covered the gun ports blown off. Clearly, whilst the use of self-sealing tanks would obviously be of benefit, nothing short of redesigning the Hurricane would make much of an improvement. All fighters were susceptible to the fire hazard; the Hurricane was worse than some.'[22]

Historian Stephen Bungay has identified combat tactics peculiar to the Hurricane which would also account for the higher fire risk:

'Most fighters hit by bombers were struck by bullets as they passed through the formation or pulled away, when they offered a far bigger target. The Hurricanes, unlike the Spitfires, would also have exposed their wing tanks during this part of an attack. The major relevant design difference between the two types is that Hurricanes had wing tanks and Spitfires did not... wing tanks were very exposed to hits from an astern attack [by fighters] whatever the pilot did. They are in the area forming the natural centre of any attacker's target area – the central fuselage and wing roots. If a Hurricane pilot flew on dead ahead (as if he were bounced and taken by surprise), there must have been a very high probability of some strikes being on the area of the wing tanks. If he saw his attacker, his most common defensive manoeuvre would have been to turn. Once in the turn, he could get out of the sights of a 109 quite quickly if he flew his machine to its limits. However, in order to do so, in banking and pulling into the turn, he would have presented an even bigger target, exposing the wing roots themselves to an attacker's fire.

The only way to avoid this would have been to bunt rather than turn, but he could not do this because his engine would cut and a 109 following him could close to point-blank range. The first few seconds of his classic defensive manoeuvre were therefore perilous for the pilot of a Hurricane in a way that it was not for the pilot of a Spitfire.'[23]

The concerns of pilots regarding their aircraft did not go unheeded, reflecting the respect the RAF had for its technically specialist, volunteer crewmen. In the aftermath of the Battle of France, and at the same time as the Linatex protection system was first being tested in fighters, the RAF had set up a committee, 'to sift available war experience with a view to seeing what lessons are to be learned which might guide future policy'.[24] Officers and other ranks from all commands were able to raise issues and concerns that they had with their aircraft or training. When the war moved to British airspace in August, the War Experience Committee actively sought out the opinions of those at its very sharpest end, despatching investigators to learn what they could from aircrew who had survived being shot down or crashing.

Squadron Leader Rees was one such War Experience Committee investigator who visited the RAF hospital at Halton during September 1940 and reported on his, 'conversations with 7 Officer and 6 Sergeant Pilots who have recently been shot down. Of these 6 out of the 7 Officers and 5 of the 6 Sergeants were Hurricane Pilots', including Nicholson, Zatonski, Page and Sutton.[25] Rees appears to have quickly taken on board the extra fire risk to Hurricane pilots, as his report made several specific recommendations aimed at improving the fire-resistance features of fighter aircraft. His recommendations, which in themselves were evidence for the slow pace of installation of self-sealing mechanisms, were:

'1. That the gravity tank [reserve fuel tank in front of the pilot] as well as the wing tanks of Hurricane aircraft be self-sealing.
2. That until all wing tanks are self-sealing the wing roots of Hurricane aircraft be blanked off.'

Squadron Leader Rees obviously went to some trouble investigating all possible factors, however minor they appeared, that could aggravate injury. Geoffrey Page testified to the difficulties he had undoing his Sutton harness because the pin was high up, almost under his chin. Page's hands had been badly burned, so releasing the pin and undoing his aircraft hood were very difficult. As soon as he released the pin he fell out of his Hurricane. He estimated that it took him 15–20 seconds to get out but that he could have been quicker but for the trouble with his release pin. His severe burns were obviously aggravated by the extra time spent in the flame-filled cockpit of his aircraft. David Hunt, a New Zealander, had experienced a similar problem with a jammed cockpit but his father owned a company that manufactured axes that could withstand high temperatures and voltages, and who insisted that his son mount one in the cockpit of his Hurricane. On 3 September Hunt was attacked by a Messerschmitt 109 and, but for his special axe, would not have been able to escape from his burning cockpit. The problems experienced by Hunt and Page led Rees to recommend:

'3. That some method of jettisoning the hood be incorporated. This especially applies to Spitfire aircraft, the hoods of which seem to jam easily and which cannot be opened at high speed. Until this has been done, pilots are advised to go into action with the hood open.'[26]

Rees' report was sent to Fighter Command headquarters on 1 October 1940, after the worst of the battle was over, but before then word had reached Fighter Command informally of the problems with the Hurricane, and a senior officer of the command requested that:

'... urgent consideration be given to the isolation of the wing fuel tank of Hurricane aircraft from the cockpit by fireproof material.

It is considered that if, during combat, the wing fuel tanks catch on fire, flames from the tanks are blown into the cockpit causing severe local burns to the pilot's leg.'[27]

The Director General of Research and Development responded on 16 October but was only able to offer a partial resolution to the issue of retro-fit fuel tank protection for operational fighter aircraft:

'I am directed... to inform you that modification action is now in hand to isolate the fuselage tank of the Hurricane from the pilot. The modification will be capable of easy application in the service but will also be applied to production aircraft.'

His news about the unsecured wing root was not so good:

'With regard to the request for isolation of the wing tanks in the Hurricane, I am to say that it was agreed by a Staff Officer of your Headquarters that although the modification already introduced in production Hurricanes to seal the centre section inboard of the wing tanks should be made available for retrospective application, such application is beyond the facilities of the service units and retrospective modification action for this sealing is therefore not being taken.'

It is worth noting that it was not just the Allied air services who were preoccupied with tank safety systems. In 1940 the Farnborough engineers had found the German tank wanting in comparison even with the unsealed British fighter tanks. It seems that German investigations of tank safety paralleled those of their British counterparts. In July 1941 Farnborough received a tank from a Messerschmitt 109F-2 which had crashed at Tenterden in Kent. That safety improvements had been made was immediately obvious to the RAE engineers. The tank was no longer metal but constructed from four layers of different synthetic rubber materials, all of which had good self-sealing properties when hit by test shots, and armour plating had replaced the bulkhead behind and underneath the pilot's seat.

By the time Rees' report was written, the tide of the Battle of Britain had turned, and the need for pilots was becoming less desperate. It was not an unreasonable assumption that as older Hurricanes were continually being replaced by the new production models it was not worth taking aircraft currently on active service prematurely out of the front line. Pilots, like Pat Wells, continued to burn in the interim, and although such casualties were no longer the manpower emergency for Fighter Command that they had been in August and September 1940, it had become as serious an emergency for the RAF Medical Service, as it struggled to come to terms with both the survival and treatment of the men who had come into its care.

Chapter Three

Above All, Alive

As burn casualties began to fill up RAF medical facilities, their prospects seemed bleak: their very survival could not have been predicted, let alone the scale and severity of their injuries. Plastic surgeons of the day were hardly ever called upon to perform the kinds of reconstruction required by tissue loss on this scale. Indeed, in 1939 there were only four full-time plastic surgeons operating in Britain (with six registrars in training). Their average workload comprised cleft palates, reconstruction of injuries sustained in car crashes (this was a growth area) and the occasional burn, although nothing on the scale of wartime injuries, and these mostly to children, epileptics or the elderly. An increasing amount of their time was being spent on straightforward cosmetic work.

Yet the situation for Geoffrey Page, Roy Lane and the others was not immediately as desperate as it might seem. For the four plastic surgeons were very remarkable men who could not have been better equipped personally to deal with the new emergency. Two of the four, Harold Gillies and Thomas Pomfret Kilner, had learned their craft as surgeons to the Royal Army Medical Corps in the Great War. Early in that conflict Gillies, the more senior man, had been alarmed by the number of face and jaw reconstructions he was being called upon to perform, and visited France to observe the pioneering work of two plastic surgeons, Valadier and Morestin. On his return to Britain, Gillies was set up at the RAMC hospital at Aldershot to develop what he had learned in France. In 1916 he received casualties from the Battle of Jutland which, although serious, were a mere dress rehearsal for his work with the men mutilated in the

Battle of the Somme. The facilities at Aldershot proved unequal to the task and in 1917 Gillies and his team moved into a specially built unit at the Queen's Hospital at Sidcup, where they received the Passchendaele casualties. By the end of the war, over 11,500 operations had been performed by Gillies and his team (which included Pomfret Kilner), consolidating his reputation as one of the founders of modern plastic surgery.

In 1918 Gillies returned to ENT work at Barts. In 1920 he completed *Plastic Surgery of the Face* which consolidated his reputation among his fellow specialists. A knighthood and lucrative private practice followed where he was joined by fellow New Zealander, Rainsford Mowlem (Kilner set up on his own). In 1930 Gillies invited his cousin, Archibald McIndoe, to join the practice. McIndoe's superb surgical skills guaranteed that he quickly became a partner in the practice despite his relative youth.

Thus, the history of plastic surgery in Britain was bound up with war, and was based on solid precedents of coping with unexpectedly severe facial traumas. Gillies had continued to consult with the Army medical authorities after 1918 and, after 1930, had brought in his partners as fellow consultants. After an introduction from Gillies, McIndoe treated several RAF officers who had contracted sandfly fever in what is now Pakistan (the fever caused severe scarring). McIndoe not only performed reconstructive surgery, but also contributed several papers to the various tropical disease journals on his experiences. Furthermore, the surgeons themselves were actively concerned with one factor in particular that would be of primary importance in the treatment of burn injuries: the viability of the grafting surface. Although grafting often took place at the end of treatment it was essential that the treatment itself did not compromise the grafting potential of the trauma area. Thus the plastic surgeon was often an active participant in the treatment process well before the patient got as far as the operating table. Gillies' expertise in grafting led him to seek to expand the scope of the process; he and McIndoe collaborated on a paper for the *British Journal of Radiology* which discussed the suitability of skin grafts for the burns and ulcers caused by X-ray treatment of tumours.

In 1938 as part of the preparations for war, all four surgeons were assigned civilian consultancies to the various military services, with Gillies in overall charge. Gillies went to Park Prewitt Hospital in Basingstoke, Mowlem to Hill End in St Albans, Kilner to Roehampton, and McIndoe to East Grinstead and the RAF. In addition to the designated military casualties, all four were expecting to deal with the predicted mass civilian casualties of German bomber attacks.

As few of Sir Archibald's private papers survive there is no way of knowing when he became aware of the scale of the problem of burn injuries. His tenure at East Grinstead began quietly; he arrived to inspect the hospital before the outbreak of war and installed his own nursing and anaesthesia team A special ward, Ward III, had been set aside for his patients, but it was some time before he received his first RAF casualty, William Cruickshank who had been shot down by friendly fire in December 1939 and had burns to his legs and back. In March 1940 Godfrey Edmonds crashed his training aircraft, receiving severe crash and burn injuries in the process. McIndoe was summoned to the RAF hospital at Halton to inspect the patient, and bought Edmonds back with him to East Grinstead. In June 1940 facial casualties from Dunkirk arrived at the hospital, many being brought directly from the coast. These casualties were primarily shrapnel or ammunition trauma cases which required reconstruction (but without the massive tissue loss of the burn pathology) and for which plastic surgeons of the day were well prepared. Edmonds, however, was another matter altogether. His entire face had been burned away and needed rebuilding. A comment of McIndoe's, made in 1958, reveals how unprepared he felt for such a challenge:

'Historically there was little to guide one in this field [of the total reconstruction of the burned face] apart from the general principles of repair perfected by British, Continental and American Surgeons. There had until then been no substantial series of cases published and none in which a rational plan of repair had been proposed. At the most, individual cases appeared in papers and textbooks on Reparative Surgery in which only too often the end result seemed to convert the pathetic into the ridiculous.'[1]

Later in the war, when asked if he had always been such an outstanding surgeon he replied:

'A good, competent surgeon, experienced, yes... but when I looked at a burned boy for the first time and saw I must replace his eyelids, God came down my right arm.'[2]

Edmonds was the first East Grinstead patient to require more than 20 operations to restore his face, after which he returned to flying and then to training some of the early paratroops.

The first time Archibald McIndoe had looked at a burned boy he had seen far more than just a formidable surgical challenge; he also saw the appalling inadequacies of existing treatment for very severe burn injuries. Because patients rarely survived serious burn injuries much before 1939, the medical response had developed accordingly for minor, rather than major injuries. The treatments that evolved during the 1920s and 1930s were clinical and chemical and rarely required surgery, so it had not been necessary to involve surgeons in the process. The principle of treatment was that of coagulation: a chemical compound was painted over the wound surface which coagulated into an encasing hide-like scab, in effect providing a chemical dressing. This had advantages on small trauma sites, 'the coagulum protects the injured area, reduces exudation and prevents sepsis'.[3] The coagulum remained on the trauma site until fresh tissue had grown underneath, at which point it was removed, much like a scab. Coagulants were a one-stop treatment, providing both first aid and long term protection.

From 1925, when they were developed by E.C. Davidson of the Henry Ford Hospital in Detroit, coagulants based predominantly on a tannic acid compound were used on burn injuries. Tannic acid, originally used in leather works to stiffen or 'tan' the hides, was continually refined throughout the 1920s; silver nitrate was added so the coagulum would dry as quickly as possible and a gentian violet compound was developed for use on burns to areas of more delicate skin, such as eyelids. By 1937 tannic acid had been refined to the point at which it could be suspended in jelly, put in a metal tube and easily applied to burns even by relatively untrained medical personnel.

Tubes of Tannafax jelly were to be found in every Emergency Medical Scheme (EMS) hospital, ambulance and medical officer's bag, as well as all RAF station sick quarters and hospital facilities – and for the few, relatively minor burns they all expected to treat, this would have been satisfactory. But, as none of them was prepared for the severity of the burning of Allied aircrew, they had no instructions for either first aid or long term treatment of such injuries and so they applied the only treatment they knew. This was disastrous. Coagulation therapy was not only inadequate for the treatment of major burn injuries but proved downright dangerous, and entirely counter-productive both to healing and reconstruction.

A number of surgeons and doctors, including Archibald McIndoe, became aware of the dangers of coagulation therapy on severe burn injuries when confronted with badly burned hands. Airman's burn frequently involved injury to the entire surface of the hand including burns which encircled the fingers and thumbs. Coagulants painted around the whole circumference of the fingers stiffened into an unyielding casing which hindered already severely compromised circulation and blocked the dispersal of post-traumatic oedematous swelling. Infection was almost a certainty under such circumstances and the coagulant would have to be ripped off and reapplied after antiseptic treatment. Apart from causing the victim terrible pain, the compression eventually caused necrosis (tissue destruction or gangrene) and the loss of substantial portions of the fingers. What tissue remained often developed heavy scarring (known as keloids in 1940, these were rope-like scars out of all proportion to the size of the trauma site) which pulled the fingers back into a kind of frozen claw. Needless to say, function of the hand was reduced to a minimum. Worst of all, from the surgeon's point of view, was the destruction to potential grafting surfaces caused by coagulation therapy. Trauma sites were enlarged and deepened by scarring and infection as well as by the removal process of the coagulum, and healing was delayed.

A burn casualty from the Battle of France was among those who endured coagulation treatment to his hands. Fairey Battle pilot William Simpson had not made it to East Grinstead when casualties were evacuated from France but had been trapped behind enemy lines in Verdun and was treated at a French civilian hospital. Tannic acid was applied to his extensive burns including those on his hands. One hand was placed in a splint for several broken fingers, and the combination of the rigid splint and the rigid coagulum was enough to rob Simpson of all his fingers. After a year spent at various hospitals in occupied France and Vichy, Simpson eventually made it back to Britain where he was immediately dispatched to East Grinstead. His hands were almost useless: 'I had one pincer grip – between the stump of my first and index fingers – and this grip had to do everything.'[4]

Geoffrey Page recalled the tannic acid used on his limbs in the Royal Masonic Hospital during August 1940:

'Then for the first time I noticed the hands themselves. From the wrist joints to the finger tips they were blacker than any negro's hand, but smaller in size than I had ever remembered them to be. I shared the V.A.D's [Voluntary Aid Detachment nurse] expression of horror… "That stuff's only tannic acid. It's not the colour of your skin."'[5]

His hands became 'tannic acid gauntlets' which were eventually removed under anaesthesia (to do otherwise would have been unbearable agony), after which the consequences of the treatment were revealed to Page and his medical team:

'I looked down at the two unbandaged objects lying propped on a sterile pillow. The pinkness of the tissue paper thin skin covering my hands made me think of newborn babies… However the joy of seeing my hands unencumbered by the crippling effects of the tannic acid more than made up for the physical discomfort. The joy was short lived. Day by day my strength increased and with it the condition of my hands deteriorated. Fraction by fraction the tendons contracted, bending the fingers downwards until finally the tips were in contact with the palms. Added to this the delicate skin toughened by degrees until it had the texture of a rhinoceros hide, at the same time webbing my fingers together until they were undistinguishable as separate units.'[6]

Just as disastrous as coagulation treatments on the hands were coagulation treatments on the face which could render the patient blind – a desperate situation given that, 'practically every airman's burn and many civilian burns show marked ectropion of both upper and lower lids, the skin loss including the eyebrows and the lash edges'.[7] When such an injury was treated with a coagulant such as gentian violet, facial tissue around the eye became stiff and immobile, leaving the patient unable to blink or to keep his eyes open for any length of time. Any damage to the eye underneath was untreatable, and the inability to keep the eye lubricated by blinking caused scratching, ulceration and infection which could damage the cornea irreparably. Once the tannic shield was removed, the scarring process set in: dramatic contraction could cause eversion (turning inside out) of the eyelids or shrinkage so that the eyelids would still not function. If the corneas had survived the tanning process, they would almost certainly be damaged by the subsequent scarring. Soon the voices of ophthalmic surgeons were added to those condemning existing burn treatments.

It had become clear as early as August 1940 that a complete reorganisation and refurbishment of burn treatment was vitally important for both patient and surgeon. Under the auspices of the War Office's War Wounds Committee, a sub-committee on burns was set up, led by Gillies and McIndoe, to investigate and make recommendations. Its report into tannic acid was delivered in a memorandum of October 1940, at the same time that Squadron Leader Rees was delivering his own report to the War Experience Committee. The sub-committee's conclusions were firm on all matters to do with serious hand and face burns. Necrosis of the fingers was definitely caused by tanning treatment, and tanning of both face and hands was dangerous and should be stopped forthwith. The report stopped short of condemning the practice altogether for minor burn injuries but noted that research on this matter was ongoing.

To publicise its findings, the sub-committee on burns organised a meeting in November 1940 at the Royal Society of Medicine where one after another the committee's members urged that, 'Tanning of third degree burns, especially of the hands and face, should be abandoned.'[8] Its star witness was Archibald McIndoe, who by November had over 20 seriously burned patients under his care. His forceful testimony against tanning burns was backed up with photographs of his patients. Few of his audience can ever have seen injuries like them, and he quickly won the support of everyone present, including the two most influential members, Cecil Waverley, senior Royal Navy surgeon, and Harold Gillies.

The November meeting was an important moment in establishing the pre-eminence of Archibald McIndoe in the field of burn treatment. As the surgeon with by far the highest number of severely burned men under his care, even in 1940, his voice began to carry the greatest authority. It was he who secured the banning of tannic acid, and it was the alternative treatments in respect of both first aid and long term care of the burn site which he had been obliged to develop at East Grinstead that became the national standard.

Tanning burn injuries was a very modern treatment: a manufactured chemical solution inside a mass-produced metal tube that could be applied to anyone by almost anyone else regardless of their medical experience. It was almost too easy, and for serious burn injuries it was not only too easy, it was counter-productive. What was needed was a return to much older, specialist, labour-intensive treatments. At East Grinstead McIndoe found himself using simple, almost classical techniques in order to maintain the viability of the trauma site for grafting by keeping it clean, dry and intact. This rejection of modern chemotherapies was very much against the usual trajectory of medical innovation; even the official medical historian for the Royal Australian Air Force noted, 'It is interesting to note that the wheel of time has made a full turn, bringing a reversion to the simple gauze and petroleum method and its variants.'[9]

McIndoe's treatment regime was the same for both first aid and long term burn wound care. Dressings of loose weave, impregnated with a greasy product such as Vaseline jelly, were carefully placed over the trauma site. Tulle gras was the most usual medium, comprising curtain net fabric cut into pieces with a '2mm mesh soaked in soft paraffin 98 parts, halibut oil 1 part [this could be omitted, depending on the rationing of fish products] and balsam of Peru 1 part'. It was stored in a metal tin and heated gently to loosen its constituent parts.[10] Sterile dressings could be applied loosely on top of the tulle gras and the entire construction could be kept moist by the application of warm saline in porous packs. The most important feature of such dressings was that they were easily removed to cleanse the wound or to prepare for surgery, without the traumatic ripping that characterised coagulant removal. Such atraumatic dressings solved many of the problems associated with coagulants; they could even be applied to jointed, functional areas such as hands, face and feet. Medical staff could look directly at the wound, which aided the early detection of infection (under coagulants the infection was hidden, usually until its smell alerted patients and nursing staff to the necrosis). Antiseptics could be applied, such as sulphonamide powder, usually blown gently over the site through a straw.

Replacing a tube of chemical cream with a labour intensive regime of nursing care was no small matter. The treatment sequence was detailed and complicated, requiring numerous specially trained nursing staff – East Grinstead had one of the highest nursing staff levels of any hospital in Britain. Red Cross Nurse Rosemary Parkes (later Rosemary Langford) joined East Grinstead in 1944 from King's College Hospital. One of the first things she noticed about her new posting was the far larger number of Red Cross nurses at work in Ward III than had been the case previously. Nurses were needed for the many daily changes of dressings, clothing and bed linen necessitated by the liquidity of the injury and of its treatment.

The beds in the ward had been redesigned with wheels so they could be moved around and with removable headrests so facial dressings could be changed from all angles. Wherever possible layered linen was used to avoid the increased risk of infection harboured by woollen blankets.

Nursing orderlies assumed a new importance in the burn ward; men were called into service who were strong enough to lift and move a severely burned patient but gentle and skilled enough to do it with the minimum of discomfort or disruption. This was not simply a question of good practice; orderlies were intrinsic to the second stage of burn treatment at East Grinstead, the saline bath. McIndoe saw regular baths in warm saline as vital to the promotion of wound health and therefore surgical viability. Immersion in the water promoted granulation (the creation of a suitable grafting surface) and kept the wound flexible – burned hands could be moved about under the water, for instance, which aided circulation and the survivability of viable joints. Dressings or clothing remnants whose dry removal would have been almost unbearably painful simply floated away when the patient was in the bath.

Like the beds the patients lay in, the baths themselves had been redesigned to maximise their efficiency and ease of use. They were made of ebonite to render them saline proof (ebonite was man-made ebony, with an enamel-like finish, expensive and difficult to manufacture). The baths had wheels fitted so they could be moved around. Complex electronics ensured that temperatures and salinity levels were constant, and the baths were earthed so that the highly conductive nature of saline would not be a problem. Orderlies lifted patients from their beds into the baths, monitored the operation of the bath and then returned the patient to bed. Bathing was done almost daily, especially if the patient was preparing for surgery, and the complexity of saline treatment resulted in East Grinstead's orderlies being among the most medically proficient of all nursing staff. The sensitivity required in dealing with this most vulnerable patient group led to close relationships developing between the two groups of men.

A Canadian patient, Leonard (Leo) Tremblay, whose injuries were caused by a crash in night flying training at the Wrexham Advanced Flying Unit on 23 May 1943, described one such relationship:

'I remember particularly one of the orderlies whose name was Johnny Ingram. Johnny treated me with respect and an uncommon devotion.

When my health condition improved and I was able to go out of the hospital, Johnny would take me out in a wheelchair into East Grinstead to the Whitehall Restaurant… We would have a few (sometimes more than a few) beers and excellent food… You see, after 57 years, these are people I shall never forget.'[11]

By the end of 1940, all McIndoe's burn patients were kept in one ward, Ward III at East Grinstead. This physical separation was in itself a radical innovation. Prior to the outbreak of war, burn patients of all kinds were kept in general surgical wards – a situation that was to say the least unsatisfactory for all parties. Infection was rife and cross-transmission between the various injury groups a certainty. Burns that were accompanied by jaw injuries were at highest risk of all (and were separated into isolation wards even at East Grinstead). The sight of burn patients could be disconcerting for other, less badly-injured patients to look at (and often to smell), as could their nursing regime. Privacy and a good deal of sensitivity aided both patient and nurse in some functions, such as feeding and oral hygiene, especially for those who had sustained severe facial injuries.

Although the burns unit was kept separate from the rest of the hospital at East Grinstead, it made full use of its other services, including pathology and microbiology labs; x-ray and photographic facilities all added to the quality of care. The hospital's original maxillo-facial remit was also of great benefit to the burned as well as the broken. Dental surgeon William Kelsey Fry and anaesthetist Ivan Magill, both of whom had trained with Gillies at Sidcup, applied their expertise to the challenge of the burned patient. To deliver anaesthetic gas Fry and Magill had developed a variety of masks that covered the whole face, thus avoiding pressure on open burn wounds. He also worked out how to administer anaesthetic to a patient who was in the late stages of fluid shift and who would need to be on the operating table for several hours.[12]

By the end of 1940, McIndoe had not only convinced the RAF and other military medical services of the merits of his regime at East Grinstead, he had also convinced the Ministry of Health. A memo was issued to all civilian hospitals and staff replacing coagulation with open irrigation techniques, and which directly referred to aircrew burns as the reason for the change:

'Burns of the hands which, in the RAF are a common injury and which have been so treated [with tannics] subsequently develop ischaemic necrosis of the fingers. This is caused by oedema development beneath a rigid crust, and gives rise to embarrassment of the digital circulation. As a result there follow contractions and atrophy of the fingers, which become useless, spindle-shaped appendages; particularly is this the case in severe second and third degree burns. Complete loss of the fingers has been noted.'[13]

Despite the speed and efficiency with which the sub-committee's recommendations were incorporated into both civilian and military medical provision, it should not be assumed that consensus had been reached on the dangers of tannic acid. This had, after all, been the chief treatment for burn injuries for at least 20 years and many physicians saw no real reason to reject it either at all or in part. *The Lancet* for the period September–December 1940 published many angry letters in defence of tanning from civilian doctors.[14] Their attitude was hardly surprising as very few civilian doctors ever saw the sort of burn injuries experienced by RAF aircrew – even Rainsford Mowlem, consultant plastic surgeon to the Army, had only seen four serious burn injuries by 1 October 1940 at his St Albans unit.[15]

There was also dissent among surgeons. In December 1940 the sub-committee had to prevail upon a celebrated surgeon of the day, William Ogilvie, not to publish an article, 'The Burnt Hand', in that month's *Lancet*, which was highly critical of the attack on tanning at the Royal Society of Medicine meeting. As a committee member wrote to Ogilvie:

'I do appreciate your kindness in not publishing the article for I feel that the treatment of burns is so much in the melting pot at the moment that the less that is printed the better.'[16]

Instead, Ogilvie's objections were made privately to the committee and were passed to McIndoe for a response. In his letter Ogilvie repeated the widely-held view that contraction of the hand occurred not because of the tanning process, but much earlier, at the moment of burning. He maintained that the position of the hands, clamped on the cockpit instruments was crucial and that they were somehow frozen in the gripping position by the nature of the flash-burn type. Despite the sub-committee's research to the contrary, Ogilvie believed the anti-tanning party had failed to appreciate this distinction and had therefore condemned tanning on flawed evidence. He stressed that he was, 'worried by the whole RAF outlook on burns'.[17]

McIndoe, who by now had all 27 airmen burned in the Battle of Britain under his direct care, made a forthright reply, calling Ogilvie's letter, 'a very dangerous piece of literature', and, 'a most unfair and incorrect statement of the situation'.[18] He was particularly contemptuous of Ogilvie's attempts to blame the type of burning:

'This is complete nonsense, and he cannot have questioned any pilot who has had this experience... A petrol flame burn is not an instantaneous flash and the vast majority of pilots whom I have questioned most carefully have an extremely vivid memory, not only of what happened, but exactly what they did.'

Ogilvie and McIndoe had a history in the matter. McIndoe ended his letter:

'He [Ogilvie] claims he has never treated a single hand burn. There he is wrong, for in fact he did treat one and that with a rigid tannic casing. Later he quoted this patient's clinical history to me entirely wrongly, not knowing that I had him under my own care at that time, and was aware of what had happened. The man's hands are among the worst of this doleful series.'

The very high level of public interest in the daring exploits of 'The Few' ensured a great deal of curiosity from the outset about what was happening to those injured in the Battle of Britain. Questions had even been raised in the House of Commons, prompting the Health Minister, Mr M. MacDonald to reply that:

'Experience in the past few months – which in the case of burns has been much wider than it could over be in peacetime or in the last war – has shown that tannic acid treatment is not satisfactory for certain types of burns. With the co-operation of the Medical Research Council (MRC) the situation is being closely watched by experts of world-wide reputation.'[19]

The work of the experts of world-wide reputation was by no means over, despite the establishment of a successful regime for treating severe burn injuries at East Grinstead. From 1941 the majority of burn patients came from bomber crews, a factor which posed two very particular problems for McIndoe and his fellow experts.

The first problem was the occurrence of injury in the environment of the bomber itself; unlike fighters, crewmen in bombers were not alone and very often first aid could be administered in the aircraft itself during flight by the injured man's crewmates. It was impossible to expect that under these circumstances the sulphonamide, tulle gras, saline sequence could be applied. First aid equipment had to be easily stored, easily transported and easily applied by aircrew. It also had to provide, 'a tolerable placebo for airmen who are badly hurt and far from home, and [which] can be used by the layman who wants to help his badly injured comrade.'[20]

Under these very particular circumstances coagulation remained the only practical and possible treatment. RAF medical officers who gave aircrews rudimentary first aid training got mixed messages from their handbooks, as the Principal Medical Officer for Bomber Command noted:

'The position at present is one of some difficulty as medical officers in their lectures on First Aid are obliged to warn aircrews of the risks of using Gentian Violet or other coagulants on such burns yet they have to admit that the only treatment available in the aircraft is the very article they are warned against.'[21]

Even Archibald McIndoe had to agree with, 'the cardinal principle of First Aid that "What will you have?" must depend upon "What have you got?"', but only on the condition that an alternative first aid preparation in tube form was researched as a matter of urgency.[22]

Fortunately he was able to draw upon the expertise of another War Wounds sub-committee headed by Leonard Colebrook, like Gillies a veteran of the RAMC in the First World War. From 1942 Colebrook led a new burns investigation unit at the Glasgow Royal Infirmary and it was this which took up the challenge to achieve an alternative for on-board first aid (previous investigations undertaken by Colebrook for McIndoe included the discovery that woollen blankets harboured infection, hence the switch to all linen bedclothes in Ward III). The ninth version produced by Colebrook's team (hence its name 'No. 9 Cream') was pronounced successful. No longer a coagulant, the thick antiseptic cream (a combination of ammonium bromide and sulphanilamide antiseptic) could be spread in the same easy way to provide first aid by loosely covering the wound and to prevent infection. To this end a special tube and spreader were also designed. The cream was approved by the RAF and issued to aircrew from the beginning of 1943. Soon after it was issued to the medical departments of the other British services, and a batch was dispatched to the US Army headquarters being set up in preparation for D-Day.

The history of No. 9 Cream is worth a small detour into the future, as the preoccupation with easily applied first aid provision for burns did not end in 1943. After the atom bomb attacks on Japan, doctors in the West tried to understand the casualty implications of this type of warfare, especially with regard to burn injuries. Archibald McIndoe himself warned that:

> '... in the next war [burn injuries] will probably outnumber all other [types]... experience gained from the steady stream of burns which were received from 1939 onwards affords little reliable data upon which we may base treatment of the deluge of burns which can confidently be predicted should another war occur... In an atomic war [burns to civilians] could be appalling in numbers and in severity and involve any member of the population.'[23]

Throughout the 1950s meetings took place at the Royal Society of Medicine and there was a Joint Services Medical-Surgical Conference in 1954, at which the subject of treating burns in large numbers was discussed. George Morley, trained by McIndoe at East Grinstead, advised that because of 'atomic flash' burns, whole hospitals would have to become burn units. Sir Ernest Rock-Carling noted pessimistically that:

'Flash burns occurring as a result of an atomic bomb and which are beyond the two-mile radius will require to be treated by individuals themselves. Extensive burns will be treated in the appropriate centres but the resources of the nation will be strained.'[24]

Once again, tubes of cream were central to the medical response to the predicted injury. As Morley advised the Joint Services Conference:

'We provided tubes of a burn cream for use as a self-help cream by aircrew in a forced landing... I feel strongly that a self-help cream such as this ought to be prepared in advance for general issue to the populace, much in the same way as we issued gas masks to the public on the outbreak of the last war and carried them about for a year or two.'[25]

Although No. 9 Cream was not issued to civilians, by 1950 it had found its way into civilian first aid posts and mobile first aid units intended for civil defence. The Home Office's *Civil Defence First Aid Manual* contained a chapter on 'Burns and Scalds' which noted that burns could be, 'caused by... the flash of a bursting bomb'.[26] The manual advised that burn victims should be taken to the first aid post or unit where they could receive treatment from:

'(iv) No. 9 Cream
     Towards the end of the last war a cream was introduced for the treatment of superficial minor burns, e.g., of the hand or forearm, and also in more extensive burns, if, for any reason, the immediate removal of the casualty to hospital was impossible.'[27]

No. 9 Cream remained part of civil defence medical provision until the late 1950s when concerns about atomic flash burns were replaced by concerns about radiation sickness.

The second problem generated by bomber crew burn casualties was one of scale. Very little adaptation had been necessary in making McIndoe's

Ward III at East Grinstead the model of best practice in the treatment of severe burn injuries. Its only shortcoming was that it was a one-off, and it had not taken either the RAF or its medical service long to realise that it could not possibly provide care for all their future burn casualties. More East Grinsteads would be needed, with the same staffing, infrastructure and ethos. The RAFMS appears to have been remarkably prescient in its plans to expand provision for victims of burns after 1940. Despite the fact that nearly all the first patients of Ward III were from Fighter Command, it was anticipated that the majority of future patients would be bomber crewmen. There is no evidence that RAFMS staff were in touch with RAF strategists planning the bombing offensive, but three out of four of the new burn units were located in Bomber Command country (at RAF hospitals in Cosford, Rauceby and Ely), with the fourth being at the main RAF hospital at Halton.

So, whilst the Battle of Britain was in its final stages, on 1 October 1940 Medical Memorandum No. TT/11/40 was issued to initiate construction of four new burn units. The new units would have at least 20 beds and the full range of facilities found at East Grinstead, including shock wards, septic wards, operating theatres and bacteriological laboratories.

The opening of the four units did not mean that Archibald McIndoe's influence diminished. On the contrary his position at the centre of what was now a nationwide burn treatment organisation was consolidated, not least because the provision of specially trained medical and nursing personnel was all done at East Grinstead. First to be trained were the four RAF surgeons who would eventually run the new units (George Morley, Denis Bodenham, David Matthews, Fenton Braithwaite), and the orderlies. Then the senior and junior RAF surgeons who would work as residents at the unit and other RAF facilities joined the hospital for six months. Nursing training was shorter, a one month attachment at Ward III before joining a unit. Nursing training was as much a question of getting nurses used to the appearance of their future charges as the learning of new techniques.[28] Despite the heavy demand for nurses at East Grinstead and the new units, there was never a shortage of applicants for the posts. Red Cross Nurse Rosemary Parkes applied in 1944 after meeting Guinea Pig Ross Stewart at a student hospital dance. Recognising a nursing challenge when she saw one, she requested a transfer which was granted and she spent the remainder of the war at Ward III. Much has been made of the attractiveness of the East Grinstead's female staff, but nurses were selected, above all, for their ability to cope with the heavy emotional load entailed by their unique charges and duties. The usual protocols of age and status were ignored – as was so often the case at East Grinstead – to allow young but gifted, capable women to assume positions of authority far earlier than they could have expected in any other hospital. Dorothy 'Waggy' Wagstaff was only 24 when she took charge of all four operating rooms at East Grinstead, finding great personal and professional success as well as a husband, RAF Maxillo-Facial surgeon, Squadron Leader Charles Dutt.

Despite the need to quadruple the number of staff qualified to treat such severe burn injuries, training at East Grinstead did not follow a formal programme. The punishing schedule of McIndoe and his colleagues made an organised timetable impossible, so a crowd of trainee surgeons trailed in his wake from theatre to ward and back again, picking it up as they went along. One of those trainees remembered that:

'... the learning process was, to say the least, arduous. This was in the main because of the enormous pressures of work, the colossal throughput of patients in the ten years 1939–1949. All of the units were overwhelmed by the demand and there was little time for systemic teaching. The hurried ward-round with one minute at each bedside, the crowded operating theatre where speed was of the essence and the immaturity of the literature all threw the burden of responsibility for learning on the shoulders of the student.

... were there no benefits for the young surgeon at that time? There certainly were. There was the sense of pioneering, the struggle to find out WHY... the haunting mysteries of the healing process. Our chiefs had the same problems and it was the close contact we had with them during the long hours of the duty rota that enabled us to absorb some detail of their techniques and some of their clinical acumen.'[29]

Construction of the burn units proceeded quickly and by October 1941 all four were staffed and ready for patients. George Morley spent two weeks at Halton, 'putting the burns centre there on the lines that Mr McIndoe wanted', before taking up his post at the Ely unit.[30] Denis Bodenham followed him to Halton, David Matthews went from Halton to Cosford and Fenton Braithwaite to Rauceby.

Surgical facilities at each unit were upgraded during 1942 so that advanced plastic surgery could be performed at the unit by mobile teams of surgeons on the ever-increasing numbers of burn casualties. McIndoe had never stopped training surgeons – 60 by the middle of 1943 and 90 orderlies – and in effect training a generation of British and Commonwealth plastic surgeons for the post-war period.[31] McIndoe treated the very worst cases himself at East Grinstead, making fortnightly visits to each unit from August 1941 until the end of the war. McIndoe had established this practice during the Battle of Britain when he toured the hospitals of south-east England, rescuing burned fighter pilots (such as Richard Hillary) from the tortures of coagulation. As he explained to the Director of the RAF Medical Service:

'I think it most desirable that I should keep in close personal touch with what is going on. In this way a certain amount of the surgery can be done by Morley and Matthews within the units and the more serious and complicated procedures withdrawn, as at present, to East Grinstead. For this purpose I would propose a fortnightly round of these Units myself in a purely advisory capacity.'[32]

As well as supervision of the new units and an increasingly heavy surgical programme, McIndoe also found himself co-ordinating research relating to severe burn injuries – work which often put him at the heart of British medical innovation. Most important was the research into bacterial infections, which could cause havoc in a burns ward, destroying graft sites and grafts, and for which there was no comprehensive answer. In 1941 an outbreak of haemolytic streptococcus meant Ward III's patients had to be evacuated to other parts of the hospital to save their fresh grafts.[33] Central to these research efforts was Leonard Colebrook and his team at Glasgow's Royal Infirmary, who undertook a huge study in the treatment of streptococcus infection in burns by Penicillin and Propamide.[34] Furthermore McIndoe was able to use Colebrook's connections to Howard Florey to the benefit of his patients:

'Professor Florey of Oxford, who has developed a technique for the treatment of infected wounds with Penicillin, has offered to supply a quantity of this substance for clinical use at Halton Burns Unit. The results of this treatment, under Dr Colebrook at Glasgow Burns Unit, appear to be most striking, and demand further investigation at

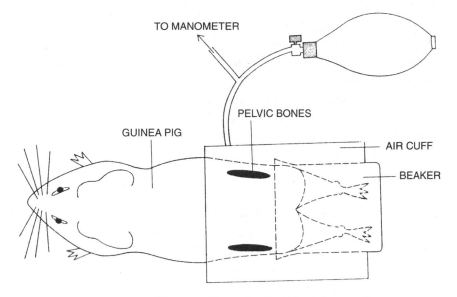

From Observations on Thermal Burns by Prof. R.A. Peters. Report 10.
The Effect of Controlled Pressure on the Formation of Oedema.

"*I distinctly heard one of 'em say: 'The way they treat us,
you'd think we were burnt airmen!*'"

Despite the increasing fame of McIndoe's patients, their real-life animal counterparts continued to perform their traditional function in laboratories – the
irony of this was not lost on this cartoonist for *The Guinea Pig*

73

Halton. However, owing to the immense expense of this substance, Professor Florey is only willing to supply it on condition that the particular technique, worked out by himself and Dr Colebrook, is followed at Halton.

It is suggested, therefore, that Flight Lieutenant Denis Bodenham, who is in charge of the Burns Unit, should be allowed to proceed to Glasgow for seven days study, under Dr Colebrook, of the technique and method of handling this important drug.'[35]

So successful was Bodenham's time with Colebrook that he later went to Oxford to assist Professor and Mrs Florey with the curing of one of the first cases of staphylococcal septicaemia. The fortunate patient, Group Captain Smythe-Piggott, who was at the RAFGH at Halton, had developed staphylococcal blood poisoning and abscesses on his lung as a result of an old leg injury.[36]

Just how widely McIndoe was recognised as the leading authority on burns was evidenced by the number of queries on the subject sent to him at the sub-committee by occupational health officers from a variety of companies including the manufacturers of Quaker Oats and various steel makers.[37] The sub-committee even passed on the more unorthodox suggestions – a South African surgeon advised that applying egg albumen and a cellophane covering was an efficacious treatment for burns. McIndoe's reply noted the privations of rationing and promised that, 'If I can find an egg in town I will give the matter a trial and let you know.'[38]

By the end of 1941, based on his experiences with the casualties of the Battle of Britain, Archibald McIndoe was recognised throughout the medical profession and the Royal Air Force as being the expert on the treatment and reconstruction of burn injuries. And by 1943 even the Ministry of Health recognised that, 'East Grinstead has a very distinct cachet in RAF circles.'[39] His reputation and that of the hospital was growing internationally, especially after pilots such as Richard Hillary and Geoffrey Page toured the United States lecturing on their personal battles. The international status of the hospital was secured when 50 American plastic surgeons were sent to East Grinstead for ten days in 1944 to train as part of the medical preparations for D-Day.[40]

It is not the intention of this book to rewrite the biography of Archibald McIndoe, but rather to connect the story of his work and its results to broader histories of Britain in the Second World War (see Further Reading at the end of this book for details of existing McIndoe biographies). With any retelling of the story of McIndoe, however, it is difficult to avoid portraying him as being something close to saintly – an inaccurate and unhelpful characterisation. McIndoe the man was no saint; he was consumed by his work as a surgeon, sacrificing much of his personal life, including his marriage and the health of his first wife, to this obsessive devotion to his patients and their care. There was a fine line between being forthright and being a bully, and McIndoe frequently crossed it. He could and did crush his own staff, his patients and their families, even his own friends and family, usually with no regard or apology for the consequences. Not for nothing was he known as 'The Boss' or 'God' at East Grinstead. However, it is difficult to see how a more tolerant, less driven man could have coped with his unique, almost overwhelming burden. The RAF's strategic bombing campaign provided him with a never-ending patient list that meant twelve-hour days were his norm, usually longer, taken up with operations that required the most careful and delicate attention at all times. At the same time he trained a generation of plastic surgeons and had to keep abreast of the latest research and development in his field. His advocacy, whether forthright or aggressive, got him past innumerable bureaucrats and other obstacles to secure the best possible care for his patients. The same energies that he used shouting at his staff could also be focused on acts of great kindness. Late one night, after a long day's surgery, he stayed up until he had organised an ambulance to bring the severely injured brother of one of his nurses from a small Liverpool hospital to East Grinstead to be treated by orthopaedic specialists, almost certainly saving the man's life. It was McIndoe the man, and we should take him all in all, who shouldered one of the mightiest burdens of the war; his daughter, Vanora, believes that in doing so he was literally worn out, dying at the relatively young age of 59 in 1960.

He formally expressed his personal philosophy regarding human reconstruction only once, in a lecture to the Royal College of Surgeons, of which he was Vice-President, in 1958.[41] The lecture gave a brief summary of the history of plastic surgery and paid homage to, 'the greatest plastic surgeon of all times', Harold Gillies. Much of the lecture is taken up with the technicalities of 'Total Reconstruction of the Burned Face' but its significance for this study lies in McIndoe's insistence on the role of the surgeon and his relationship with his patient *outside* the operating theatre. He began by noting the successful progress of plastic surgery:

'… we have now arrived at the time when… we can within a reasonable time create order out of chaos and make a face which does not excite pity or horror. By doing so we can restore a lost soul to normal living.'

To achieve, 'an acceptable result – namely a face which enables the owner to take his place in normal society without comment', the relationship between surgeon and patient, 'will often be closer than that which ordinarily exists between doctor and patient'. The relationship begins with a clear understanding between the two of what is to take place over the years of reconstruction:

'Depending on the nature of the burn, a plan is proposed at the very outset and carefully explained to the patient. It will consist of the requisite number of operations, together with time intervals between each session during which educational or training opportunities are instituted. The progressive effect of each operation is explained to the patient and an assessment made of just how much improvement he can expect from it both immediately and remotely. As far as possible the plan is rigidly adhered to by the surgeon. Thus the patient can himself plan his life between operations and a degree of confidence and trust is thus built up between surgeon and patient which I consider absolutely essential for a successful outcome both physically and psychical [*sic*]. His co-operation is essential; therefore he should understand clearly what is being done, how it is to be done, and how long it will take.'

For McIndoe, the failure of the relationship could be even worse than the failure of an individual graft, as the former had far greater long-term implications for the patient:

'At all times it must be borne in mind that it is one thing to cure the patient of his disfigurement and deformity, it is another to carry through such an arduous programme and end up with a normal human being. Throughout the surgical period and for long after it the patient will lean heavily on the surgeon for mental support, for hope and encouragement... If [the relationship] deteriorates, trust and confidence will disappear and the progression which should characterise the particular plan will also disappear.'

Above all it was his definition of what constituted a successful reconstruction that marked out the unique quality of his approach to his patients:

'... [the surgeon] should always remember that eventually any real and lasting satisfaction which this kind of work affords is derived from his own interest in what the patient does with what the surgeon achieved, rather than from the purely technical aspect of the repair.'[42]

This then was the philosophy of the surgeon who was entrusted by the RAF with its most gravely injured servicemen. But he asked much of them in return. Once he had secured the best possible medical environment in which reconstruction could take place, he set out with equal energy to secure the wider social and service environment, regarding it as being of equal therapeutic importance as the recovery ward and operating room.

There was however only one element in the burns treatment infrastructure of any significance that was not initiated by Archibald McIndoe. One year after the Battle of Britain:

'... a handful of people foregathered in a small hut in the grounds [of East Grinstead]. Some wore the uniform of the Royal Air Force, some wore lounge suits, hastily donned after a morning spent in theatre and ward; and some wore dressing gowns and bandages. The company gathered around a table in the middle of the hut where deft hands removed the cork from a Sherry bottle. Glasses were filled and raised, and as the rays of the midday sun poured through the window of the hut onto that medley of costume, on a June Sunday in the Summer of 1941, a toast was drunk to the first meeting of "THE GUINEA PIG CLUB".'[43]

Membership of the club was limited to those men of the RAF who had had surgery at East Grinstead, and the staff who treated them. There were 39 members, including McIndoe, John Hunter and Russell Davis (McIndoe's

THE GUINEA PIG CLUB

THE QUEEN VICTORIA HOSPITAL
EAST GRINSTEAD, SUSSEX

MEMBERSHIP CARD

Name... F/Lt. Truhlar   Nov. 11 194 4

anaesthetists) and George Morley. The original aircrew members were nearly all fighter pilots, including Tom Gleave, Geoffrey Page, Richard Hillary, Frankie Truhlar and Jackie Mann. The club had few specific aims, except to perpetuate the comradeship and support both patients and staff had found in each other during their time at East Grinstead:

> 'It has been described as the most exclusive Club in the world, but the entrance fee is something most men would not care to pay and the conditions of membership are arduous in the extreme.'[44]

The Guinea Pig Club was an attempt to institutionalise the unique spirit of the patient community at East Grinstead. Traditional authoritarian hospital structures and routines did not exist at the hospital (except for one – McIndoe's word was law). Officers and other ranks were treated in the same wards. Meals were not served to a strict timetable but whenever the patient was hungry. The barrel of beer kept in Ward III was a symbol of the hospital's approach but primarily its purpose was medical – full of fairly watery pale-ale it served to re-hydrate patients whose injuries could be dangerously dehydrating – and nurses found it easier to encourage the men to drink beer than jugs of untouched water. John Hunter, the chief anaesthetist, had a standing bet that if he made a

THE SPIRIT OF THE STY

patient sick after surgery, he bought him a drink. This became a Ward III tradition; Guinea Pig Peter Kydd remembered, 'After coming to after my op, I found four Pigs sitting on the end of my bed, one of whom was making a book and laying odds as to whether or not I would be sick.'[46] Ross Stewart kept a tame grass snake in his locker. Australian Guinea Pig Harold Taubman remembered waking up on his first day at East Grinstead:

'In the next bed is Paul Hart: "All right Aussie" he says, "Have a cigar" he says. Some bloke in a wheelchair, his leg in plaster, chases a nurse along the ward shouting "Taxi, taxi!" There is a lovely sound as Tim Walshe opens and pours a bottle of beer... then, the daily saline bath, and the bathroom boys, Johnnie, Eddie and their ceremonial shaving

79

DANGER ! MEN AT WORK !

GPs were encouraged to watch operations

off of my bomber command moustache and its posting back to Australia… visits to London, the Players Theatre and Whitehall nights… aah, good things happen to Guinea Pigs.'[47]

This was indeed a community of shared suffering and endeavour, which transferred the language and coping strategies of the squadron and the bomber to the hospital ward. It was also an extremely well informed community – kept up to date on their own and each other's progress by the medical team that cared for them. Patients watched actual surgeries in the East Grinstead theatre from a viewing gallery, and escorted nervous first-timers on their trolleys into theatre to give them courage. The 'spirit of Ward III' became a therapeutic agent in itself as patients looked to their fellows for support and the shared courage to face their injuries.

With the creation of the Guinea Pig Club the last piece of the burn treatment infrastructure for the RAF's injured aircrew fell into place. The process of creating such an infrastructure had begun with the burn injuries inflicted on pilots fighting the Battle of Britain – injuries whose origins lay in strategic and tactical decisions made before war began. The unprecedented severity and survivability of those burn injuries, and the esteem with which their sufferers were viewed by the entire nation, accounted for the speed and scale of the response by Archibald McIndoe and the RAF – he had built a hospital system fit for a new breed of heroes, and only just in time. After 1941 burned bomber crewmen began to arrive at East Grinstead and the four new burn units. These men came in far greater numbers and with even more severe injuries than had been the case in 1940. The Battle of Britain had provided the initial impetus but in the long run it was a rehearsal for the main drama of the bombers' war.

Chapter Four

The Bombers' War

'We've had it, and I'd rather jump than fry.'
Squadron Leader Peter Carter (played by David Niven) in
A Matter of Life and Death

On the night of 30 May 1942, Bomber Command launched the first of its 'thousand bomber' raids against German targets. The scale of the attack had an immediate impact on Cologne – and on the Home Front. 'The British public and their politicians had been almost universally awed by the scale and vision of power', of not only the sight but the idea of a sky full of huge bomber aircraft thundering away into the night on the attack.[1] The Air Officer Commanding-in-Chief of Bomber Command, Arthur Harris, was never able to muster quite so many aircraft in a single raid again, but it did not matter. Operation Millennium defined the style and scale of the bombers' war from then on. Nearly every night, hundreds of aircraft, filled with thousands of aircrew, took the war to the enemy, and nearly every night some of those that made it home landed with terrible burn casualties on board. And by an almost miraculous foresight, the doctors and surgeons of the RAF medical services were ready for them, with fully operational burn units that had been prepared months before the escalation of the strategic campaign had even been thought of.

Although fighter pilots continued to find their way to East Grinstead, from 1942 onwards by far the largest patient group came from Bomber Command. All bomber aircraft had benefited from tank protection systems from 1939 onwards. Such systems must have saved thousands of lives but they could not render aircraft impervious to the increasingly ferocious defence mounted by the Germans. Similarly, increases in the size, payload and fuel capacity of the British bomber had correspondingly increased its flammability, and the risk posed to its crewmen.

By the end of the war the Guinea Pig Club was 80 per cent bomber crew, and although RAF casualty statistics are not recorded by command, it is reasonable to assume that Guinea Pig Club membership is representative of the overall picture. The chief source for casualty figures in the services for the period is the official medical history volume on *Casualties and Medical Statistics*.[2] The volume is divided into three parts, one for each service and in each part the 'characteristic injuries' occurring to each type of service personnel are listed. The editors of the work emphasise the unique dangers of active service in the RAF over and above the other services, and the particular problems posed to the RAFMS by those dangers:

> '... the dominating problem in the RAF was the care of aircrew. These carefully selected and highly trained young men were fighting either alone, as in the case of fighter pilots, or in small units of a few men. They lived and worked in exceptional circumstances; they were submitted to the special risks of flying at high speeds, to the hazards of weather, altitude and cold, and to the perils of exposure to enemy action.'[3]

The 'characteristic injuries' inflicted on RAF aircrew are defined in the official history as, 'Burns, frostbite, immersion injuries, head injuries and certain types of fracture'.[4] Immersion injuries occurred to aircrew who had baled out into the sea or floated for days in rubber dinghies; as well as the risk of hypothermia and exposure, they also suffered from ingestion of salt water, starvation and thirst. Head injuries to aircrew were, 'a very important cause of loss of trained flying personnel', although they posed much less of a technical medical problem to the RAFMS than burn injuries – according to the official history, head injuries, 'can be expressed by the all or nothing principle'.[5] Some 97 per cent of skull fractures were fatal as were 99 per cent of skull fractures combined with other injuries. The survivors (such as they were) made a full and speedy recovery, with 74 per cent returning to flying duties within weeks, aided by bed rest and relatively simple clinical care.

The official history lists three types of fractures among the characteristic RAF injuries. Maxillo-facial fractures, usually caused by accidents rather than missile wounds, only posed a serious problem for the medical services when they were accompanied by large scale tissue loss such as from a burn. Spinal injuries, such as those caused by crash landings (harnessed or unharnessed) and parachute drops, were significant, although their treatment was relatively simple, with only rehabilitation taking any length of time. One particular orthopaedic fracture was associated with aircrew, and indeed with one particular crewman trade; foot fractures, especially of the ankle bones, were common among pilots, occurring during evasive manoeuvres or strenuous flying when the pilot's foot was, 'forcibly driven down on the rudder bar', in his efforts to control his heavy aircraft.[6]

It was burns (and frostbite – burns by other means) that were not only the most serious injuries suffered by aircrew but also required a complicated and very lengthy treatment and recovery period, often for the remainder of the war. The severity of burn injuries and all their consequences is recognised throughout the official histories, with one volume calling them, 'the dominant problem for the RAF Medical Service'.[7] Although representing only 4.8 per cent of the total injuries inflicted on the whole service (as opposed to the 40 per cent total for multiple fractures), their consequences were far more serious than any other injuries, especially those inflicted on home service personnel. Burn injuries to RAF crew abroad, whilst more numerous (7.8 per cent of injury totals) were less severe, mostly leg burns which required the attention of general field surgeons for simple grafting and less demanding nursing care.

The home force injury figures, shown in the table overleaf, demonstrate the trajectory, scale and cost of the strategic bombing campaign, culminating in 1944 with the highest aircrew injury rate of the entire air war – indeed 1944 gets its own special entry in the *Casualty and Medical Statistics* volume because of the high loss rates.[8]

The relationship between combat operations and burn injuries is demonstrated by the injury figures for 1944 being roughly double those of 1942, 1943 and 1945, matching the increasingly high-pitched efforts of Bomber Command in the strategic bombing of Germany. What is most remarkable about these figures is that as 1944 drew on, Bomber Command was increasingly diverted from its strategic mission to tactical operations to support Operation Overlord. The table also shows the prevalence of burns to functional areas, such as face and hands (headsets protected ears and shoes and socks protected feet, hence the low number of injuries to these

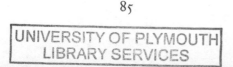

Burn Injuries to RAF Home Force 1939–45[9]

Burn type	1939	1940	1941	1942	1943	1944	1945	Total of type
Head	8	5	3	7	4		10	37
Face	7	77	123	130	113	205	170	825
Eye area	4	14	36	55	23	50	40	222
Ears			1				10	11
Neck	2	18	29	29	1			79
Chest		3	2	12	2		10	29
Back	2	2	5	10	5			24
Abdomen		2	6	2	3		10	23
Pelvic area		2	4	5	8	19		38
Arm-hand	6	97	167	204	263	478	210	1,425
Upper arm	1	23	69	82	86	178	80	519
Knee-ankle	12	91	169	195	181	292	150	1,090
Knee-hip	3	49	67	94	83	275	80	651
Totals	45	383	681	825	772	1,497	770	4,973

areas). Injuries which required the most complex nursing, surgical and rehabilitational schedules over the very long term were also the rule rather than the exception. None of this would have come as a surprise to the very highest levels of the Air Ministry; in January 1944 Chief of the Air Staff Charles Portal responded forcefully to a senior staff officer who queried the need for extra bed space at East Grinstead:

'In my opinion we must, I am afraid, expect that there will be large numbers of aircrew casualties to treat at any rate during this year, and quite possibly during next, and we may have to call upon East Grinstead to take a larger role [than expected].'[10]

The crews of Bomber Command fought their war over and beyond the front line. Without the support systems available to ground troops during first line combat, they experienced many of the same injuries (artillery, shrapnel, explosive trauma) as well as severe burn injuries that were unique to the RAF. Indeed, although burn injuries were also a feature of the non-combat environment, they were primarily combat injuries. Like all injuries to bomber crews, burn injuries did not only represent a medical problem to one specific individual; the wounded airman usually came from a badly damaged aircraft, in a way that a wounded infantryman did not necessarily represent a badly weakened unit or battalion. The severity and frequency of the injuries reveal the reality of the combat environment for its participants, and correct the misleading impression given in much of the literature that participation in bomber raids was a matter of life or death, with little middle ground. In fact, the middle ground was full of wounded men and battered aircraft struggling to get back across the front line and home.

The fact that any crippled aircraft made it out of the horrendous combat environment that existed in the skies over Germany is remarkable, and every burned crewman returned to British soil was a tribute to feats of piloting and navigational skill and courage. Such feats began well before aircraft ran into enemy defences. Heavily laden bombers had often been lurching through windy, icy skies for several hours requiring every last ounce of a pilot's concentration. The pilot's technical responsibilities posed dangers all of their own, such as the shattered ankles from feet slamming down on pedals and rudder – often pilots did not know they had even sustained a fracture until required to walk away from the aircraft once it had landed. Cloudy skies, or rain and snow, at any altitude meant the pilots often pressed their faces as closely as possible to their windscreens to peer into the sky. If the aircraft crash-landed, the pilot ran the extra danger of windscreen glass shattering in his face. Yet bad weather offered a form of protection to the raiders, as clear skies meant they presented easier targets once they ran into enemy defences.

German defences became increasingly sophisticated as the bombing campaign progressed. As well as very large numbers of anti-aircraft guns on the ground, and a well organised system of tracking incoming aircraft, the tactics of the defenders were efficient, and had very particular implications for burn injuries.[11] Alerted to the presence of bombers, Luftwaffe night fighters:

'... would carry out their search as directed from the ground, flying slightly lower than the estimated altitude of the bomber so they could look upwards for the dark silhouette of their prey against the star-light. On visually identifying a bomber they would fly below it, either to port or starboard, and fire into its wings to set the petrol tanks ablaze.'[12]

Night fighter efficiency was greatly enhanced by the addition of guns fitted to fire obliquely upward from the upper fuselage which meant the fighter could attack from directly below, in the bomber's blind spot. A Messerschmitt 110 navigator remembered:

'It was always a sinister feeling to hang only 30 to 50 metres under a Lancaster, always expecting fireworks, but nothing of the kind ever happened... I always navigated my pilot approximately 200 metres below the enemy aircraft. When about 50 metres below the bomber's port wing we opened fire, aiming between the two engines into the fuel tanks; and then we dived quickly to port to make sure the burning air-craft did not hit us.'[13]

Night fighter tactics targeting fuel tanks were enormously dangerous for British crews. Bombers had tanks along almost the entire length of their wings, and on long-distance raids, such as those to Berlin or Nuremberg, would carry fuel loads as heavy as their bomb loads. Although all bomber tanks and fuel pipes were self-sealing, no amount of protection was capable of resisting a direct, sustained blast of enemy fire. Wings were armour-plated but the extent of the armour was limited to keep weight down. The upper sides of the wings were entirely unpro-tected, so when bomber pilots undertook the usual 'corkscrew' evasive manoeuvres to avoid fighters, they exposed their vulnerable upper wing surfaces to enemy fire. The results of one such successful attack on a Lancaster were described as, 'a colossal flame stretching from the wing trailing edge, right past the fin and rudder, and of a furnace of sparks coming from a great hole in the petrol tank'.[14]

Efforts to deal with tanks and engines set on fire in this manner earned the command's crewmen two of their nineteen Victoria Crosses. During a raid on Münster (7 July 1941) Sergeant James Ward of the RNZAF (75 Squadron) was second pilot on a Wellington attacked and set on fire by a night fighter. He crawled out along the wing and smothered the flames

Air Ministry posters did not necessarily reflect the catastrophic effects fire
could have on bomber aircraft

with a tarpaulin, preventing them reaching the fuel tanks. Sergeant
Norman Jackson (106 Squadron) was a flight engineer on a Lancaster
bombing Schweinfurt in April 1944. The plane was set on fire by a night
fighter and Jackson climbed out along the wing to extinguish the flames.
Not only was Jackson wounded, he was then burned for his pains and

swept off the wing into the slipstream. He managed to open his parachute and somehow made it to the ground.[15]

Pilots could try and put the flames out themselves. They would first drop any bombs and incendiaries on board and then do:

'...a vertical dive to see if the wind force would abate the fire. In a split second the nose went down and we screamed from 22,000 feet to 15,000 feet and pulled out. This had a great effect on the fire but it didn't go out completely [Flight Sergeant Brown] told [the pilot] to do it again quickly. The nose went down again the wind noise was deafening... The altimeter showed 11,000 feet and, by a sheer miracle, the flames and sparks subsided and he pulled out straight and level at 10,000 feet with not a spark to be seen.'[16]

The raid on a Panzer base at Mailly-le-Camp on 3 May 1944 was typical. Control of the raid in the target area was lost early on, and things were made worse when an American forces broadcast disrupted the VHF radio sets transmitting the target area orders. The delay allowed German night fighters to operate at their most efficient, bringing down over 11 per cent of a 300-strong bomber attack (losses of 4 per cent were the acceptable norm).[17] The raid is often described almost entirely in terms of its losses, yet it is equally as notable for the many wounded airmen who dragged their equally wounded aircraft home from Mailly in almost impossible circumstances.

Guinea Pig Douglas Stephen, for instance, piloted a Lancaster of 550 Squadron on the raid. Fires started in the fuselage by fighter attacks spread throughout the aircraft, badly burning his hands. He kept on flying the aircraft (after 1942 bombers flew without second pilots) and, despite widespread damage, brought it down safely at Ford airfield. Stephen had returned to operations by the following year, indicating just how efficiently the RAF's burns provision had become at meeting the needs of its patients, particularly with regard to the expertise in the burned hand of Denis Bodenham at Rauceby.

Radio operator Dicky Richardson was another casualty of the raid on Mailly-le-Camp but he was not as fortunate as Douglas Stephen who managed to make it home to Britain. Richardson, before the war a postman in Worcester, was the only survivor when his Lancaster was hit on the way back from the raid. As the wounded aircraft spiralled out of control, Richardson leapt through a wall of fire to escape, only just managing to rip off his helmet – radio operator helmets had the wireless cords built in and could easily strangle the wearer in the chaos of evacuation. Although his parachute was on fire, he made it safely to the ground. Richardson's burns were some of the worst of the war, with only his feet remaining undamaged (due to his boots), but he recalled feeling very little pain. On capture he was taken to a French hospital and, after repatriation, ended up at East Grinstead. He married his fiancée, Eileen, who had waited for him, not only throughout the war but also throughout his ordeal of treatment and recovery.

Aircrew faced not only the danger of fire, but also the risk of ammunition striking them inside the aircraft, often ricocheting around before destroying as much of a human face as could a fire. Guinea Pig Harry Crombie, an air gunner in a Blenheim attacking Knappsack power station in 1942, lost half his face, including an eye, to a shell. Guinea Pig Neil Lambell was hit in the face in a raid on Berlin. He completed his mission and released his bombs without mentioning his injury to his crewmates. Lambell's fortitude earned him the DFC.

Australian Guinea Pig Harold Taubman was part of the 14/15 October 1944 raid on Duisburg. Operation Hurricane was the biggest ever night raid on targets in the industrial Ruhr.[18] His story illustrates the effects of ammunition, as well as the reality of getting home inside a wounded bomber.

'We are leaving Duisberg [*sic*] and are set upon by a Ju 88 of the Luftwaffe. After some chattering protests from the machine guns of Jack in the rear turret, the Ju 88 flies callously away, leaving three of us wounded and entirely without navigational aids to get us back to base. There is some extensive bush piloting by Peter whilst we occupy ourselves with shell dressings, making tourniquets out of intercom leads, and using morphia needles. Then finally we are over the English coast in the cold light of dawn with hardly any petrol and no hydraulics. Peter takes out his DFM with a beaut belly landing.'[19]

There were almost endless variations of ways in which bomber aircraft could threaten their crewmen. J.V. Verran of 95 Squadron was twice a Guinea Pig, once when he was hit by another aircraft whilst waiting to land after a raid on Berlin, and a second time after returning to ops during his programme of surgical reconstruction. This time, whilst returning from a raid on Königsberg (an important port for the German Eastern Front, now Kaliningrad in Russia) he was hit by a night fighter. The header tank of the aircraft was set on fire and the flames quickly spread throughout the aircraft. The damage generated a sudden loss of hydraulic pressure causing the bomb bay doors to open. Verran was sucked out of his seat and pushed up against the rear of the aircraft by the pressure change. He was held helpless as the oil fire burned his face and body. He was only released when the fuel ran out and the aircraft stalled, crashing into a Norwegian fjord. Verran and his wireless operator, fellow Guinea Pig Raymond Page, were the only survivors. Both were captured and repatriated, ending up at East Grinstead.

Returning wounded aircraft to Britain was always the most dangerous of ordeals. Crews always endeavoured to get as close as they could to the coast, knowing that ditching was not only inherently hazardous but that treacherous currents could bear the wounded in their dinghies away from safety and rescue towards the enemy or the open sea.

One such crew flew in a Wellington from 166 Squadron, led by pilot Pat Knight and with Jack Toper (later editor of *The Guinea Pig*) as wireless operator. On 30 August 1943, after a mission to attack Mönchengladbach, the starboard engine blew at 16,000 feet. The aircraft immediately went into a spin which took several minutes and several thousand feet to be corrected. Regaining course for home, the aircraft was then attacked by a night fighter, and hit by shrapnel. Knight managed to evade the fighter by a series of complicated evasive manoeuvres despite only having one engine functioning and severe shrapnel wounds in his leg – Toper remembers having to hold his leg down on the rudder bar for him. Enemy coastal defences then harried the already wounded aircraft, requiring Knight to drop the aircraft almost to sea level in order to make it home. The crew jettisoned everything on board not nailed down, including parachutes, as the one remaining engine laboured to keep them in the air. Crossing the British coast, they desperately sought an airfield but were unable to find one with their rapidly failing engine. Hoping to avoid a nearby town, Knight eventually set the aircraft down in a recreation field, where it struck a tree and burst into flames. A team from a local anti-aircraft post helped rescue the crew, but Jack Toper had been blocked from exiting the aircraft by an unjettisoned parachute which had ballooned open. The delay meant that Toper was still trapped in the aircraft when the oxygen bottles ignited, and he took the main blast right in the face and hands. When he finally exited the aircraft an eye witness described him as, 'like a living candle emerging from the plane, with flames six feet high from his face'.[20]

The interior of a large bomber aircraft was an entirely new site for a military casualty to occur. Bombers were large enough for crewmen to stand up and move about freely, rather than be wedged into cockpits, as in fighters. British bombers were designed as one large compartment so, 'RAF airmen could more easily watch each other in action and take a measure of comfort and support'.[21]

The nature of this environment was peculiarly self-reliant and isolated:

'There is little doubt… that each bomber's crew considered itself, in many ways, a separate and individual unit. No other military relationship, whether one involving superiors or dealing with subordinates, carried as much weight or was quite as critical to a man's eventual survival. The very nature of the battle waged by these crews had the effect of increasing their tendency to grow together. Bomber Command airmen flew the vast majority of their missions individually, without formation, at night, and largely out of sight of other aircraft. Many hours could be flown without seeing another aircraft. There was no single moment from take-off to landing during which they could truly relax or take their security for granted. Even the knowledge that one was part of several hundred bombers in a stream thousands of feet thick and stretching hundreds of miles ahead or behind did little to alleviate the solitary and disturbing nature of an aircrew's war.'[22]

The testimony of Sergeant Newton, a flight engineer in a Halifax, on his participation in the 1943 raids on Berlin reinforces this description of the isolation of individual bomber crews:

'There is one comfort, and it has been a comfort to me all the time we have been going over, and that is that it is quite soundless; the roar of your engines drowns everything else. It is like running straight into the most gigantic display of soundless fireworks in the world.'[23]

British crews flew mainly at night, and even in a densely packed bomber stream, their fellows, if seen at all, were large indeterminate objects against the night sky; it required care to avoid collision with them but there was no human contact. American crews flew daylight missions, and could often see other crewmen (or fighter pilots) through the windows of aircraft close to them. When British bombers were downed, other crews were unable to identify who they might be, and could speculate that pieces of falling debris were actually men in parachutes who would live out the war as prisoners. When an aircraft was hit, wounding its inhabitants, the men inside had to manage the casualties themselves, often dealing with extreme injuries such as burns or the destruction of faces by ammunition. At the same time, the aircraft had to fly on, either to or from its target, while the crew also coped with its mechanical 'wounds' and maintained constant vigilance for enemy defences or the risk of collision with other aircraft or debris.

A Canadian pilot officer on the raid attacking the Peenemünde complex (17 August 1943) graphically described the horrors of this new casualty environment. The Halifax in which he was navigator was attacked by a Junkers 88:

'We went down in a dive, trying to avoid the fighter. Then the aircraft quivered, like in killing poultry you strike the brain with a knife and the feathers release – that is the way the aircraft felt. A horrible smell of gunpowder enveloped the aircraft and the wireless operator beside me lay dying, with his entrails exposed. Then Frank [captain] issued the order, "Abandon aircraft…" he cut, and that was all. I rushed back and he was wriggling the controls without effect. They had been severed and we were spinning down.

The centrifugal force was enormous and I crawled along the floor to get my parachute. I lifted the floor hatch and the night air rushed in.'[24]

Furthermore, depending on the point in the mission when it was hit, the aircraft might be full of fuel and bombs, tanks could be on fire or leaking, and the temperature in the aircraft interior could drop below freezing. So, as well as tending to their own wounded, pilot and crew would have to cope with all these factors, which could compound injury on their own. Guinea Pig Alan Morgan's Lancaster was hit during a raid in January 1944. The rear door was blown open, endangering the aircraft and freezing its interior. Morgan lost eight fingers to frostbite in his efforts to get the door closed during which time his hands were stuck to the frozen fuselage. Only his thumbs could be saved, but Morgan was able to return to ops as a navigator and resumed his engineering career after the war.

Although unprecedented, this particular casualty environment was not unanticipated by the RAFMS. Crewmen had basic first aid training but none of them were specially trained to provide medical support. From 1943 they had on board No. 9 Cream for burn first aid, and plenty of morphia, which was considered essential for the treatment of not only the stressed casualty but also for the well-being of his fellow crew members. Wells noted from diaries how, 'deal[ing] with wounded and dying men on board one's own aircraft could push men to the limits of their endurance'.[25] George Morley commented on the use of morphine for burns patients and demonstrated the depth of understanding of the casualty environment in the RAFMS:

'The recently burned member of an aircrew is frequently a fatigued man. He may, himself, have narrowly escaped from an inferno; his associates and friends may have perished in torment. He may have fearsome memories and anxious anticipations; he may dread the future, its possibilities of disfigurement and of mutilation. The sooner he can be relieved of his memories and cares by happy oblivion, the better.'[26]

McIndoe himself had a realistic, even unflinching, understanding of the environment his patients did or would operate in. His own review of Richard Hillary's *The Last Enemy* concluded with his reflection on Hillary's death whilst training on night bombers:

'I often think of him in that last moment – his crippled hands fighting for control of his spinning plane – the cold sweat pouring from his body, the screaming crescendo of the engines, his patchwork face frozen in that mocking twisted smile.'[27]

Indeed the whole burns organisation remained actively aware of the implications of the casualty environment of the bomber for its crew. The spreader for No. 9 Cream was redesigned so that it could more easily tackle facial burns, as was the tube of cream itself, so that it could be tucked into a parachute harness in the event of a bale-out. At a meeting of the MRC's burns sub-committee in March 1943:

'Mr McIndoe mentioned the occurrence of severe chemical burns in aircrews due to splashing with the contents of Essex fire extinguishers... these extinguishers contained methyl bromide which was highly vesicant [blister causing].'[28]

After investigation by the manufacturer, the Pyrene Company, it was found that the methyl bromide aggravated any existing burn site but did not cause blistering on unburned skin. It was recommended therefore that only uninjured men used them – not satisfactory if the entire crew was burned. Indeed, the fire extinguishers themselves could pose a problem. Guinea Pig Sid McQuillan's Stirling was set on fire by a Junkers 88. He grabbed a metal fire extinguisher which itself was red-hot from the flames and which severely burned his hands. Then he was burned a second time when the Stirling crash-landed back in England.

Crewmen of bomber aircraft were not exclusively engaged on bombing raids. A large number of support flights for resistance movements in German-occupied territory were also made, which could prove just as dangerous as a threatened bomber stream. On such missions the sense of isolation was greatly increased. Bill Holmes' story of 'How I became a Guinea Pig' describes just such a mission, and the perils of the interior of a wounded aircraft. Holmes was the pilot of a Stirling on 5 July 1944, one of 29 aircraft on resistance support operations that night:

'The night of our initiation into the Sty [the Guinea Pig Club nickname for East Grinstead] was a special op dropping arms and supplies to the Maquis, and the Dropping Zone was deep into the French Haute Savoie near the Swiss frontier, in a full moon period and a bloody long solo flight. Despite stooging around for longer than was healthy, something had obviously gone wrong, and no reception committee could be seen so we set course for base.

However as we climbed from low level we unfortunately crossed an

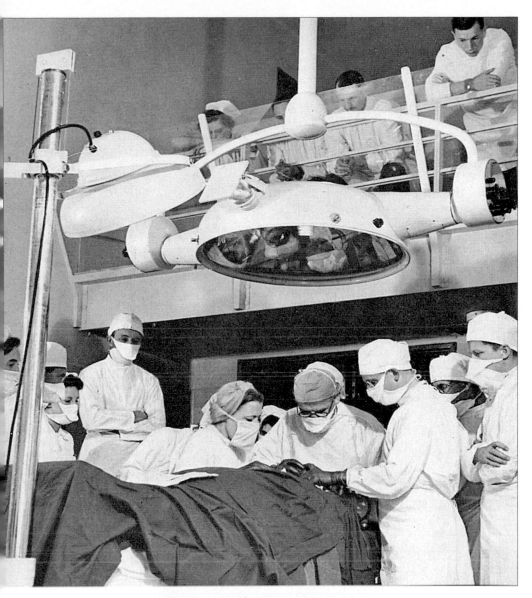

McIndoe in theatre, observed by trainee surgeons, orderlies and nurses

Canadian WDs (equivalent of WAAFs) who visited East Grinstead at their own expense every Sunday to visit patients in Ward III and the Canadian Wing

Ronald Humphreyes with nurses in the woods that backed on to the hospital, June 1942. Ronald Humphreyes was a patient at East Grinstead in 1942 and 1943 following an accident at his Northern Ireland Fighter Squadron which resulted in him losing an eye, aged 20

In August 1942 Ronald Humphreyes returned to his Spitfire Squadron 504. He took this picture of himself on a MkZC fighter leaning on the housing of a 20mm cannon, using a delay on his camera

John and Betty Bubb with Tony at the outset of the war

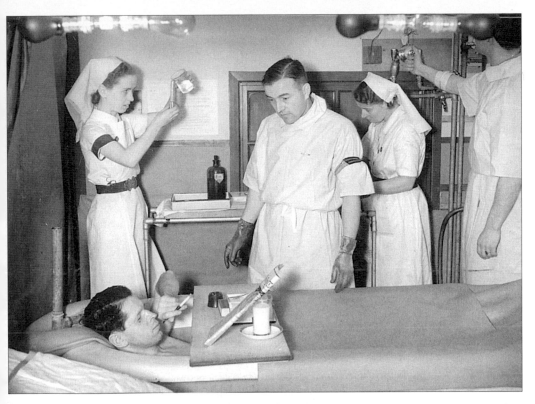

Chief orderly Cyril Jones oversees the saline bath, 1942

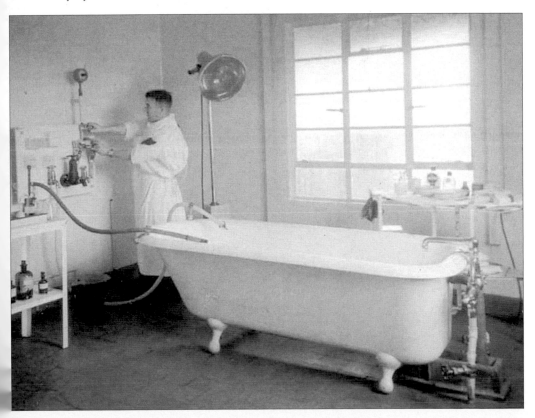

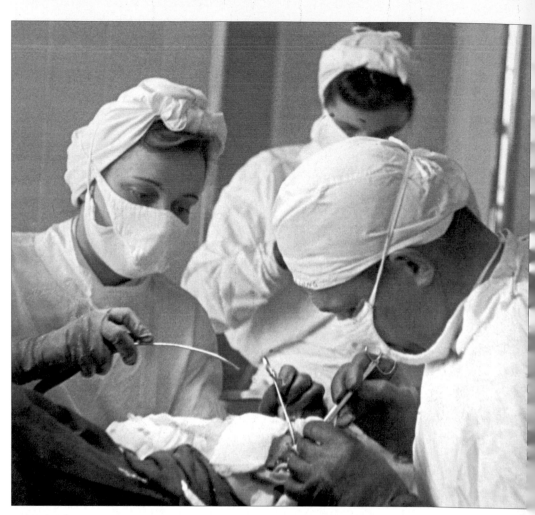

The intensity of theatre at East Grinstead

Major David Charters on joining the
RAMC in 1938

Theatre nurses outside Ward III

Charters (centre, wearing a tie) and his medical staff at Bad Soden

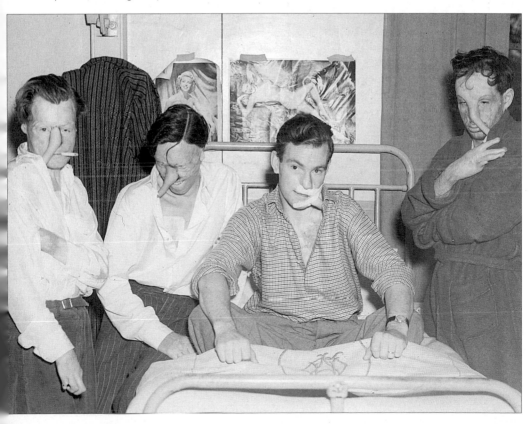

The immediate results of reconstructive surgery – which needed to be so carefully explained

Nurse Rosemary Parkes, here in her Red Cross uniform, was typical of the young, determined (and often, beautiful) women who rose to the challenge of nursing McIndoe's patients at East Grinstead

Patients and nurses outside the Annex

1944: One of the many parties at the Marchwood Park Convalescent Home

Patients and nurses enjoying the summer of 1944 outside Ward III

John Hunter (far left), chief anaesthetist, with patients and nurses

Christmas in Ward III, 1944

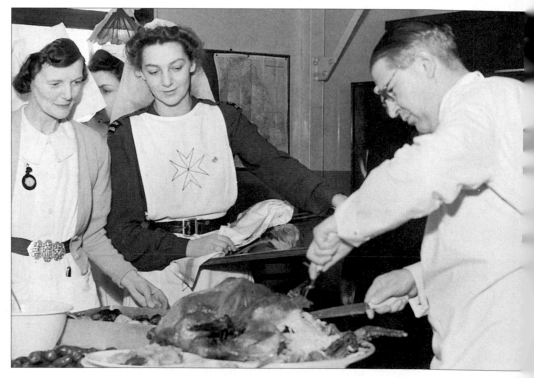

McIndoe, in surgical scrubs, carves the 1944 Christmas turkey

McIndoe joins his patients at the Whitehall

Jack Allaway, Bill Foxley, WSC, Claude Allen and Ricky Rix with Winston Churchill, August 1946. During the visit Churchill was concerned that suitable crockery for burned hands be used, and watched his guests carefully as they drank their tea

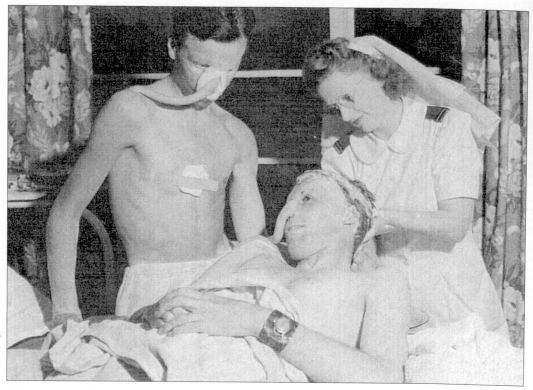

Bill Foxley (standing) in the second stage of his pedicle graft. This would become his new upper lip. With him is the Canadian patient Stu Duncan and Canadian nursing sister Mons Stapleford

William Foxley's Wedding Day, 28 June 1947. From left: John Hunter, McIndoe, Bill's parents, RAF Surgeon Squadron Leader Jerry Moore (Foxley's best man, who worked on his face and particularly his hands), unknown bridesmaid, Bill and Catherine Foxley, little sister Pat, the Bride's parents, Matron Caroline Hall, and Theatre Sister Jill Mullins

Dorothy Wagstaff in her office at East Grinstead

RAF Surgeon and Squadron Leader Charles Dutt marries Theatre Sister Dorothy Wagstaff in East Grinstead

		POST ⚜ OFFICE	4	At	Sent
No.		**TELEGRAM**		To	COPY
Office Stamp	EAST GRINSTEAD SUSSEX 11 DE 41	For free repetition of doubtful words telephone "Telegrams Enquiry" or call, with this form, at office of delivery. Other enquiries should be accompanied by this form and, if possible, the envelope.		By	
		Originating Subr.			s. d.
				Charges to pay	

SQD/LDR AND MRS DUTT THE DORSET ARMS HOTEL EASTGRINSTEAD =

MAY THE WAGSTAFF GRAFT TO DUTT BE A PERFECT TAKE
AND YOUR FUTURE THEATRE OF OPERATIONS BLESSED
WITH HAPPINESS = THE THEATRE STAFF +

Prefix	If CDE	Handed in	Office of Origin and Service Instructions or Nature of Service, if other than telegram.	Words	Received
		9.21 AM	EASTGRINSTEAD T	31	From At DMD
51-4806.			CHARGES on Imperial and Foreign Telegrams and Radiotelegrams. £ s. d.		By A24

1952 Reunion pre-dinner
group at the Whitehall

Dinner, later that same
evening

The 1960 Staff Christmas Party at the Camden Town Marks and Spencer. Jack Toper (with pipe) and Mrs Jack Toper (extreme right)

Bill Foxley, Jimmy Wright and Henry Moore with 'Reclining Figure' from Moore's Summer 1961 show at the Marlborough Fine Art Gallery. The opening night benefited the RAF Benevolent Fund

A reunion of the Canadian Guinea Pigs

In 1990 the Battle of Britain Memorial Flight dedicated a Spitfire to the Club

The Guinea Pig Club Reunion,
September 1999

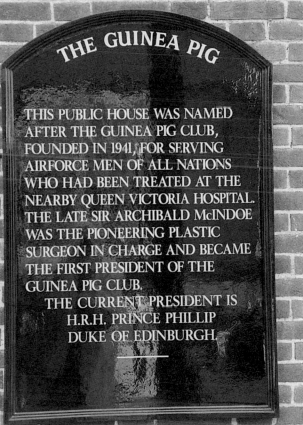

THE GUINEA PIG

THIS PUBLIC HOUSE WAS NAMED
AFTER THE GUINEA PIG CLUB,
FOUNDED IN 1941, FOR SERVING
AIRFORCE MEN OF ALL NATIONS
WHO HAD BEEN TREATED AT THE
NEARBY QUEEN VICTORIA HOSPITAL.
THE LATE SIR ARCHIBALD McINDOE
WAS THE PIONEERING PLASTIC
SURGEON IN CHARGE AND BECAME
THE FIRST PRESIDENT OF THE
GUINEA PIG CLUB.
   THE CURRENT PRESIDENT IS
   H.R.H. PRINCE PHILLIP
   DUKE OF EDINBURGH.

A town's fitting tribute

The boys who came to East Grinstead from all over the world

airfield and all hell broke loose. Flak ripped into us, destroying throttle and pitch linkages, put both inner and port engines u.s., holed the petrol tanks and set fire to the port wing root which we were able to extinguish. After checking that we were all OK, and dribbling rather than bleeding, we clawed our way back up to 8000 feet on a runaway starboard outer, 28,000 revs on the starboard inner, and 2 dead port engines. A sitting duck for night fighters, but luck was with us and we staggered on unmolested. By this time we were awash in high octane and getting more and more intoxicated on the fumes, which gives rise to some very funny, peculiar and disjointed conversations. Since the fuel gauges were registering empty, ditching in the Channel became a distinct possibility, but as I am a lousy swimmer and Thorney Island came into view, I decided to put her down if possible. Then the octane intoxication came into play, I forgot that a left hand circuit would entail turning into two dead engines and of course instead of lining up with the flare path we plunged into and across the main runway. With everyone in crash positions, Harry Stannus and I both heaved with all our strength pulling back on the control column, somehow we greased the aircraft in on its belly, wheels up and in one piece.

However, as we skidded along, we crossed the tarmac and up she went and "Red Hot Mamma" [the crew's unfortunate nickname for their aircraft] lived up to her name. After coming to rest Harry pushed me out of the pilot's escape hatch and was horribly burned as a result of the delay in getting himself out. After falling off the top of the aircraft, I found that I had somehow lost my flying boots and socks and I remember vividly that the grass was wet. I also remember that ammunition was exploding so it was time to go. Sadly, Chalky White, our navigator, didn't get out and was burned to death, but the rest of us survived… an experience which some of us can never forget, but from which we emerged, hopefully, better, more tolerant men and very proud members of our world famous club.'[29]

It was not just the combat environment which so threatened aircraft and airmen. Factors such as weather, runway construction and technical failure were at least as threatening as enemy fighter defences. Aircraft were at risk the moment they left the ground – in fact take-off was a particularly precarious time as heavy aircraft were full of fuel and bombs, posing a threat not only to their crews but also to ground personnel. As pilots strained to lift their aircraft off the ground they could be imperilled by all manner of dangers, beginning with the runway itself, which was often dangerously degraded by the sheer volume of heavy bomber traffic, aggravated by poor drainage.[30] Such sub-standard runways caused a number of problems for aircraft, not the least of which was the threat to tyres. Guinea Pig Bill Warman was a flight engineer on a Stirling, which had a tyre rupture, slamming debris against the undercarriage and causing a petrol tank to explode (the same chain of events caused the Concorde disaster of July 2000). Warman was not only badly burned in the crash, he also swallowed large amounts of petrol and required surgery for both internal and external injuries. Henry Standen was awaiting take-off in a Hampden for mine-laying operations in December 1941 when the wing tips of his aircraft touched another Hampden, discharging a burst of static electricity. Both planes burst into flames, and Standen was badly injured when an oxygen bottle exploded, destroying his right eye. Despite his injuries, he did manage to get away from the aircraft before the mines and bombs exploded. And the dangers of take-off never diminished: Guinea Pigs John Harding and Bill Anglin were due to make a mail flight in a Dakota in January 1945 but following an aborted take-off their aircraft exploded. Their injuries were exacerbated by the highly flammable nature of their cargo. Harding wrote later, 'all I can recall was that giant blow torch effect as the port inner fuel tank burst inside the fuselage.'[31]

Certain aircraft types were more inherently dangerous than others, either by construction or in that they were simply out of date for the type of campaign being waged. The Stirling bomber was withdrawn from front-line Bomber Command service in early 1944 as it was simply unable to attain or maintain sufficient altitude to be protected by the bomber stream (the Stirling loss rate during 1943 of 6.7 per cent was deemed unacceptable). Similarly the Halifax Marks II and V were withdrawn for the same reasons after a disastrous raid on Leipzig on 15/16 February 1944 which saw the highest losses of the war so far.

Worst of all was the Avro Manchester medium bomber which failed its pilots on almost all counts. Its Vulture engine was underdeveloped, giving it a poor rate of climb, and frequently cut out altogether when near the aircraft's ceiling (which was below even the earlier Hampden's maximum of 20,000 feet). The hydraulics were unreliable, its undercarriage was weak and collapsed on heavy landings and, 'under each engine nacelle ran a Y-shaped coolant pipe that proved lethally vulnerable to local shrapnel bursts'. 207 Squadron was founded to test this calamity and among their number was Guinea Pig Les Syrett, who was terribly injured when his Manchester crashed on take-off in June 1941. He broke his neck in two places, his back, his shoulder blade, his elbows, wrists and all the fingers on his left hand. Syrett wrote of his experiences on the testing programme where, 'crashes and forced landings were a daily occurrence'.[32] He was one of very few survivors, and only because his engine cut out on take-off at 150 feet, not at 10,000 feet. He died in 2002, still angry about the lives wasted by the Manchester.

Of course bomber aircraft did not have a monopoly on severe aircrew injuries. As the war went on, East Grinstead received patients from all the RAF's various commands both home and abroad – and for some, crashing in water, rather than crashing in flames, could have equally devastating consequences. At the age of just 20, Derek Martin was appointed second pilot of a Sunderland flying boat, at the time one of the largest operational aircraft in the world. Based at Oban in Scotland, Martin and his crew flew constantly on anti-submarine patrols and convoy escort duty as the Battle of the Atlantic took an increasingly heavy toll on Allied shipping. Missions were long and stressful, staring down at endless grey ocean waves, although the presence of Sunderlands acted as a deterrent to the U-boats seeking to attack the convoys. At the end of what could often be 12 hours of flying time, the pilot had to negotiate his 25-ton aircraft on to the most precarious landing site in the entire service: the floating flare path. Three boats were lined up at 600-yard intervals, each with a strong battery-powered light on the masthead, and positioned so as to give as good as possible an indication of the wind direction. The lights would only be switched on when the aircraft due to land appeared overhead and fired a coded signal. The pilot was expected to line up with the flare path, touch down between the first and second boat, and settle in the water before reaching the third. Even in good weather, the pilot usually needed a couple of runs before making a successful landing, and very calm seas could be just as dangerous as rough ones, making it impossible to judge height. Bad weather and fog multiplied the dangers of both calm and rough landings.

Still not yet 21, Martin was given command of his own Sunderland, and he and his crew continued their gruelling schedule of escort and anti-submarine patrols in freezing temperatures, appalling weather and at risk from attack by enemy aircraft. On 14 March 1941 Martin and his crew were called out to investigate reports of a U-boat operating south of Iceland. Despite the fact that they had only just returned from a 12-hour mission (ten of them at night) and had been given no time to sleep, they set off again for another 12-hour round trip. Some 600 miles and four hours later, they had found nothing and began their return to base. Visibility was poor, the night was dark, cloud was low, fog was forming and the sea was dead calm, but Martin was at the limits of his fuel capacity and so a diversion to a safer landing area was out of the question. Flying over Oban he saw the three lights of the flarepath through the fog beneath him. After two failed attempts at landing, Martin believed he had got the approach just right, but the combination of fog and the flat sea made it impossible to judge the height of the aircraft, and rather than land on the water, the Sunderland ploughed under it.

Martin's first reaction was relief that the relentless roar of the engines, which were located only feet from the flight deck, had stopped. To this day he is not quite sure how he exited the stricken and sinking aircraft – he remembers an hallucination at one point where he saw himself strapped in his pilot's seat – but he was eventually hauled out of the freezing Atlantic into a rescue launch. Martin's injuries were so bad his rescuers threw a blanket over him, assuming he was dead. Their attitude was all too understandable: Martin's scalp had been almost entirely ripped away from his head, his skull had been damaged and his left eye hung out of a torn and smashed socket. His 'corpse' was left on the quayside at Oban while the rescuers tended to some of the living casualties, but when signs of life were seen, desperate efforts were made to revive

Derek Martin in London, aged nineteen, shortly after the outbreak of war

him. The local surgeons patched up his head and scalp and, as soon as he was strong enough to be transported, Martin was sent to East Grinstead.

By the time of his arrival, the repairs to Martin's skull had started to degrade, so as well as performing the permanent grafts required by the scalp tissue, McIndoe had to find a way to ensure that the foundations of the repairs remained sound. Once again, the relatively simple application of saline irrigation did the trick, albeit through an elaborate system of draining tubes which kept the area under the scalp clean and surgically viable. From Martin's point of view, the only snag was that he had to lie stock still on his back for several days so that the tubes remained in place.

After his first bout of surgery at East Grinstead, Martin was sent for a period of recuperation. This enforced rest from flying did not suit him at all, and he made his way to the Coastal Command HQ where, despite the heavy bandaging of his head and face, they attached him to a flying boat operational training unit. On his return to East Grinstead, McIndoe was furious. After a further series of operations, Martin returned full time, and with permission from all the relevant authorities, to operational duty. In 1944 Martin took up one of the more unusual posts of the war at that time: he became chief of staff of the joint-services forces occupying the Cocos Islands in the Indian Ocean. His main responsibility was to oversee the construction of airfields for future heavy bomber operations over Malaya. He was the only such chief of staff from the RAF and received the OBE (Military) for his work in the post. Martin is not just the only Sunderland boat captain in the Guinea Pig Club, he was also a founding member, thus ensuring representation for the men of the Battle of the Atlantic as well as the Battle of Britain.[33]

Air stations were dangerous places in general, not just for the crews of aircraft attempting take-off or landing. Australian Guinea Pig Johnnie Hill was an 'erk' – a ground-crew member – who was waiting one sunny March afternoon for the return of a Typhoon training squadron. Although not as dangerous as the Manchester, the Typhoon was known to have a problem with engine cut-outs during take-off. Hill was reading a newspaper with the other mechanics in a dispersal hut when:

'... one of my companions... gave an urgent cry, "Look out!" From his position he had seen a Typhoon bounce out of control several hundred yards away, travelling at about 200 mph making straight for us, and realised that the next bounce must plummet the machine into our midst... There was a thunderous ear-splitting roar as the aircraft slammed into the building. Immediately 160 gallons of aviation fuel exploded in a tumultuous searing flash. It may have lasted from ten to fifteen seconds, it seemed an eternity. I reeled under the awful heat, my newspaper added to the inferno and I thought "this is it, this is death". Then as suddenly as it came, the roaring and the searing was over... I was still walking around in a numbed, dazed condition, my feet seeming not to touch the ground [when] rescuers began to arrive, and one airman commenced to beat out my smouldering overalls, unintentionally causing great pain to a burn on my left knee. My

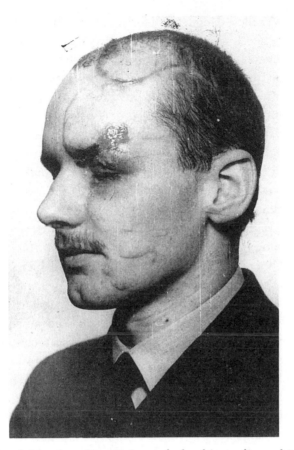

Derek Martin at East Grinstead after his crash, aged 21

hands were black, with a numbness and an icy feeling. I saw with horror the skin forming great black folds, like loose fitting rubber gloves, and I knew instinctively that I would lose all the skin from my hands. From the expressions of the rescuers around me, who were doing all they could to help us, I gathered my face must have also been a ghastly sight.'[34]

Almost all Hill's fellow mechanics were killed or badly injured. He was sent to an RAF hospital where McIndoe found him on one of his fortnightly trawls and brought him back to East Grinstead. Similarly, Guinea Pig Johnnie Weston was badly burned at his Filbeck station when a damaged Lancaster hit the buildings, killing 64 and injuring many others.

Perhaps the cruellest danger of all for aircrews was that of fog. Runways that had been perfectly clear when bombers left for Germany could become invisible and impenetrable on their return, when the crew were almost certainly exhausted from their efforts and might be wounded. Fog hid not only the runway but also other aircraft already landed or crash-causing debris. Guinea Pig Tom Gleave saw just this problem at first hand after he had taken command of RAF Manston, a fighter station in north-east Kent, midway through his surgical reconstruction programme. Manston's coastal location meant it often received damaged bombers which were unable to make it back as far as their own stations and were forced to land on Manston's short fighter runways. On 28 August 1942 damaged bombers returning from raids on Nuremberg and Saarbrücken arrived at Manston, unaware in the fog that 45 Spitfires were parked down the runway. Three Wellingtons and a Stirling got down safely but a second Stirling crashed through several of the fighters. A third Stirling hit even more fighters, littering the runway with debris and rendering it unusable for several hours while it was cleared. Incidents such as this forced the Air Ministry to re-examine a moribund project to research fog dispersal techniques.

The FIDO programme (Fog Investigation and Dispersal Organisation) was born in 1942, under the watchful eye of Winston Churchill's chief scientific advisor, Frederick Lindemann, and indeed of the Prime Minister himself who was kept appraised of progress in regular reports from his 'Prof' and from Chief of the Air Staff, Charles Portal.[35] What appear to have been unlimited resources were thrown at the problem and a huge programme of research undertaken (including the requisitioning of the Earls Court Ice Rink in London). During 1943 FIDO systems of burners along runways were installed at 16 RAF stations and the first was used at Gravely in November, saving four Halifax stragglers from a raid on Leverkusen. From then on, FIDO proved its worth many times over, saving lives and aircraft that might otherwise have been lost. FIDO, like East Grinstead, sent out a strong and clear message to the RAF aircrew that everything possible was being done to secure their safety and recovery behind the British lines. Beyond them, however, was quite another story.

Chapter Five

Beyond Ward III: Canadians and PoWs

In time for the worst casualty year of the war, the RAF had ensured the creation of four medical sites where its burned aircrew could receive the treatments, both short- and long-term, their severe injuries demanded. At all these facilities McIndoe's regime defined the care such casualties received as soon as they were removed from the crash site. The speed at which this regime was applied was crucial, as any delay meant the wound surface was compromised and the risk of infection greatly increased. Both these factors diminished the capability of surgeons to graft quickly and efficiently, and meant extra demands on the resources and staff of the burns unit, as well as threatening the preservation of function in the burned area. Mortality rates increased also as treatment was delayed.[1]

Once the casualty was removed from the crash site to either a civilian or military medical station, treatment for primary and secondary shock would be administered, as well as pain-killers. Whilst taking responsibility for stabilising the patient, at this stage medical staff kept their interventions to the injury itself to a minimum. Their interventions were based on the instructional memoranda from Archibald McIndoe and the RAFMS forbidding the use of tannic acid derivatives on burn injuries, and advising the application of tulle gras or saline compresses as a first aid measure.[2] The memoranda emphasised that no further action should be taken and called for, 'the earliest removal [of such casualties] into special burns centres.'[3] 'Earliest removal' meant within a maximum of seven hours, and accordingly burn casualties were given priority in both

motor and air ambulances.[4] Only on arrival at the burns centre did the
patient receive the 'sulphonamide, tulle gras, saline sequence' (and/or
saline bath treatment) from trained staff that would ensure maximum
tissue viability.[5]

The location of the RAF burns centres ensured that many casualties
could be transported there directly, although this was not always the
case. Guinea Pig Ian Craig, who crashed whilst flying a reconnaissance
flight over the French coast in a Wellington, was taken to Southampton
General Hospital which was closest to his crash site, but moved immediately to Ely RAF Burns Unit (where there was room for him) for treatment on his burned face and lost eye. It should be remembered that

"DON'T YOU THINK THAT'S A LITTLE *TOO* GOOD?"

during this period there was relatively little road traffic, so ambulance journeys from many English bases could be made to one of the centres well within the seven hour time-frame. Burn patients were also given priority on air transports, in recognition of the time sensitivity of their injuries.[6]

As the war progressed and all units gained experience in treating the thousands of injuries generated by the bombing campaign, surgeons and doctors trained at East Grinstead spread skills and expertise across the whole organisation. Denis Bodenham, for instance, the RAFMS surgeon trained by McIndoe to head up the Rauceby burns unit, became an accepted authority on the treatment of the burned hand. Patients could therefore move between East Grinstead for their facial reconstructions, and Rauceby for attention to their hands, lightening the load on both. Archibald McIndoe's daughter, Vanora Marland, remembered that this was a distinguishing feature of her father's professional style. He moved rapidly around East Grinstead, always trailed by a group of trainee surgeons (he told her, 'I like the hounds at my heels') and was delighted when he could send patients to a former trainee whose expertise now matched or even exceeded his own. But always it was East Grinstead, and McIndoe, at the heart of the care given to burned aircrew, and there were two sites in particular – one very close to Ward III, and one rather further away in every sense – that demonstrated the very real practical and psychological importance of one surgeon to this extraordinary group of warrior-casualties.

The Canadian Wing: 'vast gifts... from Canada'[7]

At every Guinea Pig Club reunion dinner, held annually in September, the Guinea Pig Anthem is sung. The last verse is as follows:

> We've had some mad Australians
> Some French, some Czechs, some Poles.
> We've even had some Yankees,

God bless their precious souls.
While as for the Canadians
Ah! That's a different thing.
They couldn't stand our accent
And built a separate Wing.

Prior to the assembly of forces for Operation Overlord, the largest group of overseas servicemen based in the British Isles were from the Royal Canadian Air Force (RCAF). RCAF personnel were widely dispersed in RAF formations throughout the country, some in RAF squadrons and some in squadrons of their own (although confusingly these also contained some British airmen).[8] Canadians had arrived to serve with British forces from the very outset of the war, together with men and women from the other dominions – it was a Canadian fighter pilot, John Gillespie MacGee, who had written perhaps the best poem of the air war, 'High Flight' ('Oh, I have slipped the surly bonds of earth...'). And there had been Canadians among the earliest members of the Guinea Pig Club. Flight Lieutenant Gordon 'Freddie' Frederick was on the first club committee, and submitted the inaugural 'How I became a Guinea Pig' article for the very first edition of the club magazine.[9]

In view of this wide dispersal of their servicemen, the Canadian authorities had decided against creating a large-scale, bespoke hospital system. In general, the medical needs of their aircrew and casualties were met within the existing medical system of the British Isles. Only two units were run uniquely by and for the RCAF: one at Bournemouth was used largely by the aircrew selection board and to test and train crewmen for night vision work, the other at Warrington served as a repatriation depot. From 1941, according to the official history of Canada's war, 'the principal scene of RCAF hospital activity in the United Kingdom during the Second World War was at East Grinstead in Sussex, some twenty miles south of London.'[10]

This was hardly surprising, for just as burn injuries were the dominant problem for the RAF's medical services, so it was for their Canadian equivalents, and as RAF burn casualty numbers mounted, so did those of the RCAF. Indeed, so significant was the percentage of burned Canadian aircrew arriving at East Grinstead that, as early as 1941, the medical service of the RCAF dispatched its Principal Medical Officer (Overseas), Group Captain Ross Tilley, to a permanent posting at the hospital. Captain Tilley had some preparation for his post, having trained with one of only five plastic surgeons based in Canada before leaving for his British posting, and upon arrival at East Grinstead struck up an instant and lasting rapport with Archibald McIndoe. So great was the trust that existed between them that when McIndoe took his only break from work at the hospital to have abdominal surgery in 1943, Tilley was given overall charge in his absence.

McIndoe, Tilley, Hunter (Chief anaesthetist at East Grinstead)

Tilley's first few months at East Grinstead were spent brushing up the plastic surgery techniques he had learned in Canada, trailing McIndoe round the wards as so many of the foremost plastic surgeons of the post-war period would do in their turn. Tilley was given permission to build his own Canadian team of specialists around him. The arrival of an anaesthetist, three specialist nurses and two all-important orderlies meant that there was now a fully-trained operating team at East Grinstead, and in July 1942 the first all-Canadian plastic surgery operation was performed.[11] During 1942 this team handled all the Canadian casualty cases they could, but this was rapidly becoming an ever-diminishing proportion of the increasing number of RCAF casualties. Not only were there not enough hours in the day for Tilley and his team, there was not enough bed space in Ward III itself. It had become obvious to all at East Grinstead that nothing less than a bespoke Canadian wing would solve the problem.

The Canadian government secured permission to fund and build such a wing, dispatching a special unit of Canadian sappers to undertake the work. Agreement was immediately forthcoming, not just because the work would incur no actual cost to the British authorities, but for other reasons as well, discussed in correspondence between Harold Whittingham, Director General of the RAFMS, and Louis Greig, Air Secretary at the Air Ministry:

'The RCAF are very anxious to develop a Burns Centre of their own within the confines of the EMS Hospital at East Grinstead, and I feel that we should not place any difficulties in their way in attaining their end, as the provision of this permanent building of 50 beds would be an advantage to East Grinstead after the war, and at the same time allow a large number of cases of burns to be treated at East Grinstead during the forthcoming operations in Northern Europe...

As things are progressing quite satisfactorily on the Canadian behalf, I suggest that we neither paddle or use the rudder but let them drift in the direction they are currently going. It will make the Canadians happy to have this hospital and will do nobody any harm; though, strictly speaking, we are supposed to provide and control their medical and hospital treatment in this country. Their proposal will not affect our prestige and if they feel that it raises theirs, it is all to the good.'[12]

The new wing cost $80,000 Canadian and, due to some delays in procuring building materials, took a year to complete. On an inspection visit the chair of the Ministry of Health's finance and building committee noted that it had 50 beds, nine of which were segregated for infectious cases, two saline baths and was, 'beautifully equipped, most of this equipment having come from Canada.'[13] The staff establishment was duly increased from seven to 51, including medical clerks, lab assistants and chefs (a key part of any maxillo-facial team as great care was required in preparing meals for men with shattered jaws and facial burns).

Tilley ran the Canadian wing along exactly the same lines as McIndoe at Ward III, sharing the New Zealander's convictions about the very particular nature of care required by such casualties, and the need for his most personal attention (nurses in the Canadian Wing remembered how he would go up to the hospital at 11 p.m. on his bicycle from his digs above the Whitehall pub to visit men he had operated on early in the day). This aspect of treatment at the Canadian Wing was considered so important that it received due and unique attention in the pages of the official history:

> 'The work at East Grinstead ran the gamut of the field of plastic surgery. In addition to the surgical work, the staff gave considerable thought and effort to the psychological aspect of the treatment of severely burned and deformed personnel. The patient's mental attitude was closely watched. To combat the lowering of morale, to which so many of these patients were prone, the staff discussed a patient's case with him in order that he might adopt a more objective attitude towards his disability, and directed attention to making the patient's physical and social environment as agreeable as possible. The latter point was thought especially important.
>
> A cheerful outlook was regarded of paramount importance in leading the patient to a realisation that he need not become a recluse, and giving him the courage to meet the general public once again. Efforts were made to reduce military discipline to a minimum and to provide the comforts of home... So successful was the work of the staff from both a surgical and psychological point of view that approximately 80 per cent of the aircrew patients recovered sufficiently to return to flying duties.'[14]

All the stories of how airmen gained their Guinea Pig Club membership provide valuable insights into the nature of the war fought in the air, and the patients of the Canadian Wing were no exception. 'Freddy' Frederick, the Canadian committee member, qualified for membership twice (or as his fellow club members put it, qualified for a bar to his Guinea Pig card). He had been burned in a fighter squadron in 1941, and then on his return to operations as a Mosquito observer on D-Day he:

> '... ran into a spot of trouble over our target and got badly shot up. We made it as far as the Channel and then hit the sea about 7 miles off Dieppe. We hit at something like 260mph and bounced. I just had time

to brace my feet against the instrument panel and get the escape hatch open, while Tony, my pilot, pushed out a distress call, before we hit again, this time at about 110mph.

Instead of going out through the top escape hatch, we were somewhat surprised to find ourselves making a door right through the bottom of the aircraft. It was a somewhat novel and undignified exit but it got us out. I had quite a bit of trouble getting clear of the tangle of wires etc., and was under long enough to get several good swallows of the stuff that England rules, and generally wish I had been a better boy and kinder to my mother.'

Despite facial and leg injuries from the shrapnel fired at their aircraft, Frederick dived back into the floating Mosquito and rescued the pilot who was strapped into his heavy armour-plated seat. They both managed to get into their dinghies and paddled away, as the aircraft sank.

'Then we heard a Mosquito coming in low. Tony had lost the safety light out of his Mae West and mine was u/s. I still had my flashlight on a string around my neck but it had a heavy mask over it, to dim it right down. I got it off in time, but jerked a tooth out of my denture doing it.'

His attempts were wasted as the Mosquito failed to spot them. Instead they began drifting towards Dieppe and potential capture. They decided not to paddle until morning and to concentrate on staying warm. The following day was spent paddling northwards and trying to attract the attention of RAF bombers raiding the coast of Dieppe. Finally they were spotted by two Spitfires which orbited above their little dinghies warding off marauding Messerschmitt 109s until the air/sea rescue Walrus seaplane arrived. Frederick soon arrived back at East Grinstead for his second set of remedial works.

Leo Tremblay's military career was short lived. Posted to No. 17 (P) AFU advanced training unit in Wrexham for fighter pilots in May 1943, he crashed during his second solo night flying exercise. The aircraft burst into flames around him on take-off, and he suffered third degree burns to both hands, both legs and, 'a slight scorching on nose and chin.'[15] From Wrexham Emergency Hospital, which treated his severe impact injuries, Tremblay was transferred by air ambulance to Ward III and the care of

Ross Tilley. Neither Tilley nor McIndoe was able to save Tremblay's shattered and burned right leg and it was amputated at thigh level. Tremblay returned to Canada as an invalid in 1944.

Ronald Noon-Ward was a navigator with 199 Squadron, whose task was to provide jamming screens against German radar to protect Allied bombers. His account of his membership qualification gives a vivid picture of the last moments inside a wounded aircraft:

'On March 5th, 1945 we take off on our 15th operation at 1642 hours from RAF Station Northcreake, in a Stirling EX-E headed for France. This is a Mark III Stirling which can reach an altitude of 18,000 feet, a 3,000 feet improvement over its previous brothers.

We arrive on station over Metz and commence our racetrack course and have been radiating our very strong jamming signals for about half an hour when suddenly a tremendous noise hits our starboard wing, and the aircraft tilts violently to port. I climb up to my astrodome and see that between the inner and outer starboard engines there is a hole of about six inches in diameter and flame is shooting out of it just as it should from a blowtorch. Both the bomb aimer and I report that the whole wing is afire and without hesitation, Tiny, our pilot orders the crew to bail out.

With that I whip off my helmet and oxygen mask and take my chest pack from its wall rack and being very careful not to open it inside the plane, clip it on to my harness. I then clamber over the very high main spar obstruction toward the rear and note that George, our Rear Gunner, and Tom, our Electronics Specialist, are already on their knees opening the floor exit hatch. I also note that visibility is decreasing for two reasons: the fuselage is filling with smoke, and our Mid-upper Gunner has accidentally opened his parachute inside the plane and it is billowing all over the place and he is desperately trying to gather it up...

I am trying to decide whether to go out through the side door, with its inherent danger of being cut in half by the tail plane, or via the floor hatch, when I suddenly feel a severe stinging pain on my face and then a tremendous pain in the groin as if someone very large and very strong had kneed me, and the third sensation is absolute silence. Then I realise that I am floating to earth on my parachute. The aircraft has exploded.'

Noon-Ward had literally been blown clear when the aircraft exploded, suffering bad facial burns as well as his other injuries. As he descended towards the French countryside he realised his suit was on fire but then he fell through some heavy cloud and the dampness put it out. He landed, was picked up by Allied forces, and eventually made his way back to East Grinstead and the Canadian Wing. Bomber Command records note that only one Stirling was shot down on 5th March, and that was by the 'friendly fire' of an American artillery unit.[16]

The Royal Canadian Air Force was also responsible for bringing some of the first American airmen into the war in Europe and thus for giving the Guinea Pig Club all its members from the United States. Ray Leupp was injured in a Hurricane when it crashed and his face was smashed against the instrument panel. After the war Leupp returned to his native Ohio and qualified as a vet, naming his practice, the Marchwood Animal Hospital, after Marchwood Park where he and the other Guinea Pigs went for rehabilitation in between their operations. When the American weekly magazine *Collier's* carried a photo story, written by Martha Gellhorn, about East Grinstead in May 1944, it led with a picture of Leupp captioned, '... an American member of the RCAF who, after two years of treatment, has a new face and new hands and is ready to fight in the European skies again.'[17]

Holebrook 'Hoke' Mahn's aircraft crashed in the sea, stranding him in a dinghy for almost a week, and forcing him to kill and eat a seagull to survive (causing much ribaldry when his fellow Guinea Pigs heard about his ordeal). During treatment for his badly burned hands and injured legs, Mahn married an East Grinstead nurse, and their wedding made the front page of the *East Grinstead Gazette*.[18] Ward Bowyer, who suffered some of the worst burns even McIndoe had ever seen, completed this select group. After his treatment was over, he remained in Britain and pursued his dreams of a career as a writer, enrolling at Cambridge to take a long overdue degree in English literature (and acting as deputy editor of *The Guinea Pig*). Bowyer's courage and determination were thwarted when he died of a stroke in 1949 during his studies.

The prestige that accrued to the RCAF medical service by its association with McIndoe and East Grinstead ensured that all its aircrew based in Great Britain had heard of the work done at the Canadian Wing. For two men in particular, the reputation of the Canadian Wing did as much to save their hands and faces as did the work that was actually done there. André Browne (RCAF) and Alan Smith (RAF) ended up in an RAF hospital facility in Wales where, exceptionally, the medical officer in charge treated their burn injuries directly, without referring them to East Grinstead. After relatively minor surgery had gone wrong, Browne was told his fingers and most of his hands would need amputating, and Smith was given a similarly grim prognosis. Smith was told confidentially by a nurse at the hospital that he ought to be at East Grinstead. So, exercising his right as a Canadian, he demanded to be moved. An ambulance was duly summoned and the relevant appointments made. At the last minute, Browne climbed on board and the two of them set out. Smith was taken immediately to the Canadian Wing and, when Tilley and McIndoe saw Browne's injuries, the ambulance returned to Wales empty. Both men's hands were saved. Browne recorded his, 'gratitude not only to Canada for the treatment he was given at the Canadian Wing, but especially to one Canadian in particular', in the pages of *The Guinea Pig*. Alan Smith related the story of their narrow escape for a Canadian TV documentary crew in 2001.

By 1944, when they were to be most needed, East Grinstead – Ward III and the Canadian Wing – and the four satellite burns units represented the most formidable and effective response to burn injuries anywhere in the world, backed up by the total commitment of the RAF to its treatment regime. But all the efforts made on behalf of RAF aircrew had one thing in common: they were only available to crews in Britain. In the combat environment of the European skies, the men of Bomber Command were on their own. They alone confronted the chaos of the interior of a wounded bomber, where relief was often several hours and hundreds of miles away. Worst of all, for some of their injured comrades, that relief was not just hours but years away as they found themselves not just casualties but prisoners of war as well. Yet, extraordinarily, McIndoe's authority in the matter of their burn injuries could be felt even across the front line into Germany itself.

Meerschweinchen in den Lagern
(Guinea Pigs in the Camps)

Ten thousand RAF aircrew were taken prisoner during the Second World War, many of whom were from downed bomber aircraft. Few of the very severely injured aircrew survived for very long after capture. Apart from the extreme rigours of being shot down, crashing or landing by parachute, German treatments for shock and transfusion techniques were a decade out of date, and what medical attention there was often did not begin until after survivors had been processed in transit camps and then sent to the main PoW camps.[19] But crewmen did survive – men like Johnnie Johnson, a Canadian crewman on a Halifax shot down in May 1943, who sustained injuries so bad he was the subject of a propaganda broadcast by Lord Haw Haw.[20] Frazer Falkiner was another. An Australian fighter pilot who had flown escort on the mission that dropped Douglas Bader's prosthetic legs on St Omer hospital, Falkiner had been shot down and found himself in the very same hospital before transfer to a PoW camp. All these men became patients in a surprisingly efficient medical organisation, given that it was inside the PoW camp system in Germany, but one which was staffed almost entirely by Allied medics, many of whom had been captured during the fall of Greece and Crete.

One of those was Major David Charters (PoW No. 23911), a surgeon with the Royal Army Medical Corps who was captured in Greece in April 1941. Entirely by accident, Major Charters found himself at the centre of burns provision for PoWs in Germany and there are remarkable parallels between his story and that of Archibald McIndoe at East Grinstead. Both Charters and McIndoe shared the same ambivalent view of authority, especially to authority not receptive to their demands. Similarities in their family backgrounds go some way to explaining this attitude. Both men were of Scottish Presbyterian stock: McIndoe, having been born in New Zealand, was disinclined to humour British snobberies; Charters, born in Stirling, came from a long line of Scottish missionaries (and was named David Livingstone for the most famous of his uncle's colleagues). He had begun his practice in Birkenhead, earning the name of 'the Poor Man's Doctor' because he so rarely charged fees to his more needy patients. His social conscience earned him the trust of the dock workers during the General Strike of 1926 when he was one of very few doctors allowed to cross the picket line.

Like McIndoe, Charters had no idea of the severity of the injuries he would end up treating in the PoW camp medical system. He was not trained in plastics but in ophthalmics, and there can have been little in his pre-war practice that would have prepared him for the reconstructive work he was called upon to perform. After his capture Charters was transferred from a Greek PoW hospital to the camp hospital (*Lazarett* in German) at Stalag IXA Kloster Haina to treat captured servicemen with eye injuries. This was a large hospital with orthopaedic and ophthalmic wards as well as a workshop to make and mend artificial limbs. There was a particular need for ophthalmological skills as many of the PoWs in work camps were used for quarrying and stone work, resulting in frequent eye injuries due to dust on the cornea. The hospital facilities included a large magnet supplied by the International Committee of the Red Cross (ICRC) for drawing out metallic particles.

Because of Charters' expertise in repairing eyes, he was sent all Allied aircrew with injuries not only to their eyes but also to the general eye area. Charters' willingness to assume responsibility for men with burns to their eyelids in particular was of the greatest possible importance to his patients as eyelid burns almost always led to blindness if untreated, even if there was no initial damage to the eye itself. Despite the fact that he had 'no experience in peacetime' Charters proved an able plastic surgeon, and from 1943 was sent PoWs with general facial injuries as well. At the same time as receiving this new and challenging patient group, Charters' relationship with the camp commander was disintegrating. A Red Cross report of August 1943 into worsening conditions at Kloster Haina noted the lengths Charters was prepared to go to ensure the best possible care for his patients:

'[All the British officers at the camp] unanimously supported... the points put forward by the Senior British Medical Officer, Major D.L. Charters, as to why the position in this Lazarett has become so serious. None of the doctors feel able to carry on with a heavy and difficult task unless there be a complete change of policy on the part of the German Commander, who, it would appear by well-founded statements and proofs, is putting every possible obstacle in the way of the British doctors and their staff… Since [Dr Jung] has taken over the former atmosphere of understanding in the Lazarett has disappeared and made room for a continuous state of uncertainty and insecurity, having a most damaging effect on the arduous work of the British Doctors treating over 400 Grands Blessés [seriously wounded].

In the first place the British doctors suffer from the utter insecurity of administration. This point was stressed with all the vehemence at his disposal by Major Charters. He declares not being able to carry on in this kind of atmosphere, looking after the hospital and doing fine ophthalmic operations where all the time there is the threat by some unfounded order of the Stabsarzt [senior German doctor] his work may be completely nullified, be it by the premature discharging of patients or by yet another break of the Geneva Convention or possibly by imposing a new collective punishment on the prisoners.

Major Charters protests most vehemently against Dr Jung's discharging at random and without hesitation patients who are in the middle of treatment and without asking Major Charters' expert opinion, all this simply as a matter of reprisals… Major Charters pointed out that so far there had been contravention in the case of [Articles 9, 11, 13, 42, 46, 48 of the Geneva Convention].'[21]

Charters' courage in criticising his conditions had a remarkable effect. After a visit and intervention by the ICRC Kloster Haina was closed down, many of its patients were repatriated, and the remainder, including the medical staff and officers, were transferred to Stalag IXB, at Bad Soden, a spa town. Major Charters, who had turned down the opportunity to be repatriated with his patients, now found himself the chief medical officer of a larger hospital, formerly a sanatorium, well located on a country hillside with good facilities and a convent of nuns in one wing of the building. Like McIndoe, he now had complete control of his environment and, within limits, the co-operation of the authorities. Charters established extremely friendly relations with Oberfeldarzt Dr Boerst (the German Chief Physician). A second ICRC delegate noted:

'Major Charters confirms that he has full control of everything and is able to run the lazarett as he pleases. The German Oberfeldarzt interferes in no way and is well disposed towards the British and US patients and their staff.'[22]

It was as well that Major Charters found himself in the much improved facilities of Bad Soden. The injury peak of 1944 was as much a feature of Charters' patient load as it was for Archibald McIndoe and his surgeons in the four RAF burns units. Charters reported to the ICRC:

'... the proportion of prisoners of war now arriving at this lazarett suffering from burns of the face and contraction of the skin is rather higher than at any time previously.'[23]

Between October 1943 and March 1944 Charters performed over 150 plastics and eye operations with very few, ageing surgical tools. During March 1944 the camp, which by now was officially designated as the centre for British and American PoWs with facial or ophthalmic injuries, was visited by ICRC delegate Gunnar Celander who noted:

'On the first day of my visit I discussed with Dr Charters the conditions at the hospital, and on the second day I handed him the valuable instruments worth more than a thousand Swedish kronor... the doctor was delighted and most grateful for the instruments and as he was unpacking them he said that he would now be able to perform various very delicate operations... 150 operations have been performed here since October, last year. A large number of plastic operations have been performed recently on burned faces... the hospital made a very good impression on me. The British M.O. devotes himself entirely and seriously to his work.'[24]

Werner Buchmueller, a second ICRC delegate also praised Charters' efforts:

'Again the Delegate of the Protecting Power [Switzerland] admired the skills with which Major Charters has performed difficult plastics operations, grafting skin etc. Some of the results are astonishing.'

What was equally astonishing was the range of services that the ICRC was able to offer the PoW medics and patients in their care. Many of the PoW doctors took professional examinations whilst in captivity, with the ICRC providing text books, examination papers and results from the various professional bodies to the camps. One such candidate was Archibald Wright Thomson, also an RAMC ophthalmic surgeon captured in Greece, although he never met David Charters. Thomson:

'... managed to collect enough cases to write a thesis for my MD in Germany. I can paint a little and I managed to illustrate it with watercolour drawings of the Retina etc. The watercolours were provided by the Red Cross who sent us lots of "Occupational Therapy." Bless them and the Geneva Convention.'[25]

Thomson was successful in gaining his MD, and had clearly taken advantage of the environment he found himself studying in; his thesis was entitled: 'Vascular Abnormalities in the Eyes of Young Servicemen'.

There were limits to Charters' independence. Although he secured extra weekly rations for his charges in the form of an extra half litre of milk, an egg and 50g of honey, he was unable to secure sufficient supplies of clothing – urgently needed because burn patients were often delivered to him with few clothes on, their own having been burnt off. He applied constant pressure on his Oberfeldarzt and wrote many letters to the ICRC on the matter, also requesting more dressings and yet more replacement instruments as he had no means to sharpen existing stocks. This was hardly surprising as in six weeks over March and April 1944 he performed 30 operations. The visit by the Red Cross delegate reported that, 'most of these... are consisting of skin graftings after burns of the face... most of the results are really excellent.'[26]

During this period Charters and McIndoe encountered each other, albeit indirectly. Mrs Bromley Davenport of the ICRC Invalid Comforts Section visited East Grinstead to seek McIndoe's advice as to what materials should be shipped to Bad Soden. The results of that meeting were recorded in *Prisoner of War* magazine, a monthly publication sent to all next of kin (and which, for the sake of encouraging PoW relatives, erred somewhat on the side of optimism):

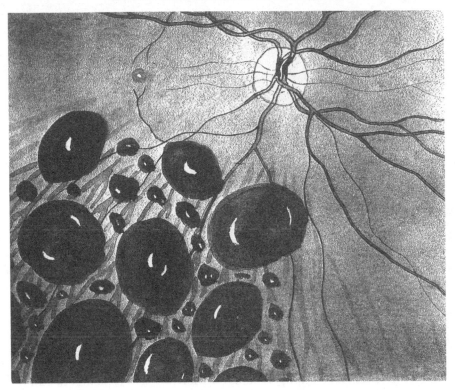

'Scarring of the Retina' – an illustration painted with Red Cross watercolours
from A.W. Thomson's M.D. thesis

'Airmen shot down in enemy territory who may be suffering from
severe burns on hands and face stand a good chance of escape from permanent disfigurement, for there are prison hospitals at which British
surgeons are equipped to perform the necessary skin-grafting operations according to the latest method.

The work of Invalid Comforts Section has made this blessing possible. In collaboration with Mr Archibald McIndoe, head of the RAF
plastic surgery centre in Sussex, sets were compiled of the highly specialised equipment and dressings, and these have been sent with
detailed instructions direct to the hospitals concerned. Not only is the
patient's future recovery thus cared for; everything possible is being
done to relieve their present pain. Special silk lined gloves, for
instance, are supplied by the Section for the men's burned hands,
which are acutely sensitive until the new skin grows. Even cigarette
holders find their place in the hospital stores.'[27]

More detail about this encounter emerges in an article in the same magazine in its last edition of July 1945:

'Plastic surgery has played a major part in the war against pain and disfigurement; and here again prisoners in Germany were not forgotten, and the Invalid Comforts Section was able to send them the necessary equipment...

Great help was given in obtaining instruments quickly by Mr McIndoe, official plastic surgeon to the RAF at Victoria Hospital, East Grinstead, who got his own instrument maker to deliver emergency equipment. This equipment was sent off by the Red Cross by air, made the journey in record time and enabled two eager surgeons [no records exist as to who the second surgeon was] to carry on their plastic work.'[28]

One of Charters' patients, Jack McEvoy (44 Squadron, Bomber Command), remembered that Charters worked from diagrams and notes drawn up by Archibald McIndoe to guide him in the delicate and crucial grafting of replacement eyelids. McEvoy was fortunate in that, having had his jacket burned off, Charters was able to find him a thick woollen sweater despite the clothing shortages. McEvoy also remembers climbing on to the roof of Bad Soden to paint a large red cross to warn Allied bombers not to attack the medical facility. He also recalled Charters' intense focus on his work, his dedication to his patients – Charters had after all refused repatriation – and his reserve. He never called his patients by their Christian names and, although McEvoy mentioned their shared Scottish background, never made small talk with him. He trusted McEvoy, however, giving him a gold watch for McEvoy to pass on to his wife Margaret back in Birkenhead when McEvoy was repatriated in March 1945. Charters was clearly a gifted surgeon: McEvoy's eyelids were considered so good that he required very little work on his repatriation to Britain and so he never joined the actual Guinea Pig Club (although he is on the mailing list for *The Guinea Pig*).[29] Another PoW patient, Maurice Butler, noted that, 'all of us were really Guinea Pigs at Bad Soden where the eye surgeon did his best to help us by a correspondence course from East Grinstead'.[30]

Former Chairman of the BBC, Marmaduke Hussey, also met Charters when he ended up in Bad Soden with serious leg and back wounds. Details of his imprisonment and treatment are in his autobiography but he too remembers Charters as brave and dedicated but always formal to the point of coldness. The young Hussey had hidden about him some bullets and a compass which he insisted on passing to Charters before he was repatriated to Sweden, in case Charters should wish to escape. Charters accepted them with due gravity but presumably never used them as he stayed on at Bad Soden until the very end of the war.[31]

Charters also treated one of the most unusual members of the Guinea Pig Club: Vladimir Razumov, known to fellow club members as 'Raz the Red Guinea Pig'. Razumov was a Soviet fighter pilot, who was shot down over Novorossisk and badly burned. Rather than dying in the brutal camps of the Eastern Front, entirely by accident Razumov found himself in the gentler PoW system dealing with Western prisoners, ending up at Bad Soden where Charters performed several operations on his eyelids. Jack McEvoy also recalls the Russian being taught basic English phrases, mostly profane, by the other patients in the recovery ward. At the end of the war, in a further act of dedication and courage, Charters had Razumov dressed in a RAF uniform and taken back to Britain, where his injuries ensured his immediate removal to East Grinstead. A little older than the average club member, Razumov was remembered by the East Grinstead staff as a courteous and charming man, who comforted a young nurse who had burned her hand on a metal teapot, despite his own terrible condition. Razumov was never allowed to complete his reconstruction; in July 1946 two burly Russians turned up at East Grinstead to visit him and he was never seen again. All efforts to trace him by the Guinea Pig Club have proved fruitless.

In addition to performing complex and demanding surgery, Charters co-ordinated the rehabilitation of blinded PoWs, establishing a Blind Centre at Bad Soden with equipment sent out by St Dunstan's via the ICRC, so that Braille lessons might be taught, and preparations made for a sightless future. From January 1945 Charters' surgical schedule increased almost daily ('we are fairly near to the West, that we are receiving fresh batches of casualties from the hospital trains'), and he was once again forced to use dulling blades and dwindling supplies of dressings ('a month's supply of dressings can be used up in a single day') until the camp's liberation in May.[32] Charters' courage and ingenuity were recorded in the official New Zealand history of the war which noted that he had managed to contact the American forces advancing on the town of Bad Soden to request that they occupy the town without further shelling as damage had already been inflicted on both the hospital (despite Jack McEvoy's painting efforts) and the surrounding buildings.[33]

Not all captured Allied aircrew were as fortunate as those men who found themselves under David Charters' care, first at Kloster Haina and then at Bad Soden. Guinea Pig George 'Tubby' Taylor flew in a Wellington which crashed in the North Sea leaving him with a face full of flak. He spent the next three years in a series of PoW camps, ending up in Stalag VIIIB in Silesia. He endured a death march of 500 miles before repatriation took him first to RAFGH Cosford and then to East Grinstead.

Canadian Larry Somers' war ended:

'... on 2nd June 1942 while flying a Spitfire over the English Channel on his 110th mission. His aircraft, one of a group of 47, on a fighter sweep, encountered 30 enemy fighters and in a very short while the Spitfire's petrol tank was hit. He and 11 other Spitfires, split from the main group, decided to make for home but were attacked again by another set of Nazi fighters. Bullets poured into the cockpit igniting the petrol lying there from the previous dogfight and the aircraft became a blazing inferno. The plane plunged towards the sea and, although blinded by smoke, he managed to extricate himself from the burning aircraft before it hit the water. Submerged in parachute silk, Larry was able to release the rubber dinghy and clambered aboard, only to drift helplessly as he found it impossible to use his badly burned hands and arms on the dinghy's paddles. Two days later he was picked up by a German motor launch.

Larry was taken to Boulogne and then to St Omer hospital where he remained for three weeks under the care of German doctors. From there he went to a prison camp hospital and was eventually transferred to a total of 10 camps, the first four being hospital camps. By refusing to divulge any information other than his name and number the second hospital punished him by not changing his dressings for five days... He was later moved to a hospital staffed by British doctors [at Bad Wildungen near Kassel] who discovered, while changing a dressing on the left side of his head, that there was a bullet hole through the top of his left ear...

When the Russians began their advance from the east, Larry and thousands of other allied prisoners were forced to walk 150 miles on foot and then travelled three days in a truck, and as the Allies came in from the west, they were forced to march another 200 miles back again.'[34]

Somers was eventually repatriated to East Grinstead where Ross Tilley remade the eyelids originally repaired for him in the camp by an RAMC medic captured at Dunkirk. No records exist as to who this man was.

Alois Siska was, like Tubby Taylor and Larry Somers, a member of both the Guinea Pig and Goldfish Clubs (for those who had been saved by a dinghy) as well as being a member of the Free Czech Air Force, 311 Squadron. When his Wellington's port engine caught fire, the plane crashed in the sea and the four surviving crew members launched the dinghy, despite dangerously heavy seas. In the crash, Siska's legs were badly burned and injured. For the next five days, the survivors battled heavy seas which swept them away from rescue. The pilot and the navigator died, leaving Siska and the front gunner alone. Eventually they washed up on shore only to discover it was occupied Holland where they were promptly captured. Siska's injuries were so severe – the ordeal in the dinghy had also caused severe frostbite – that the German military doctors decided to amputate his legs. Fate took a hand when he went into cardiac arrest on the operating table and it was decided to treat him using less radical methods.

After six months of treatment at a German military hospital in Holland, Siska was moved to Germany, but not for him the relative stability and safety of the PoW camp system. Instead, as a Czech who had fled Czechoslovakia, he was sent back to Prague where he was charged with high treason. From there he was sent to Colditz to await court martial. By a bizarre twist of fate, Siska's case was deferred due to the log jam of prosecutions generated by the assassination attempt on Hitler. Instead, still injured, he was moved to another camp for injured PoWs, leaving Colditz one day before the American forces arrived to liberate it. When Siska's own camp was itself liberated one month later, he was repatriated to Brussels and then to the RAFGH at Cosford, which immediately arranged for him to be transferred to East Grinstead for treatment to his shattered legs and feet.

Siska was the last surviving Czech Guinea Pig and hosted visits of the Guinea Pig Club to Prague. In November 2002, during a NATO meeting in Prague, the British Prime Minister, Tony Blair, asked to meet him and the other surviving members of the Free Czech Air Force. Siska died in 2003 and his obituary, like those of so many other Guinea Pig Club members, appeared in the *Daily Telegraph*.

David Charters finally went home to Britain with his patients in May 1945. Like all returning PoWs they were processed at RAF Cosford, where 55 of his burn patients were referred for further plastic surgery work either at Cosford's own burns unit or at East Grinstead. It is a tribute to Charters, who treated most of them, and to the other nameless medics who did their best in the worst of circumstances, that the number was relatively low. In addition to resuming his ophthalmological practice in Birkenhead, Charters became the official doctor to Tranmere Rovers Football Club (although he had season tickets at Everton) and at the Liverpool Boxing Stadium. A quiet man before the war, his family remember that he became even more reticent and austere on his return, deploring any kind of ostentation, triviality and, particularly, the waste of food. Charters only rarely mentioned his PoW experiences, although his family realised that his imprisonment was the most overwhelming event in his life. He wrote of his experiences only twice, producing a small (now lost) leaflet describing how to improvise medical tools from ordinary objects – a testament not only to his working conditions but also to his practical nature – and an article for *The Lancet* of January 1946 in which he reported on the case of a 'Gunshot Wound of both Orbits'. This article was the only instance where he ever referred to the privations of surgery in a PoW camp, where, without an anaesthetist or assistants, he performed a complex and delicate procedure using a local anaesthetic on the patient.[35]

Many of his colleagues in the post-war period never even realised his history, but when they were contacted as part of the research for this book, none of them was surprised at Charters' courage and determination, or by his ability to adapt his surgical skills in the most testing of environments. Charters had clearly been greatly admired – even loved – by all who worked for or with him for his gentleness, his clinical abilities and flair (despite his skills being somewhat old-fashioned) and his quiet Christian convictions.[36] Charters' reluctance to capitalise on his war experience led to him declining an invitation to Buckingham Palace to collect his MBE which was instead sent to him by registered post.[37]

Chapter Six

The Trustees of Each Other

'We are the trustees of each other. We do well to remember that the privilege of dying for one's country is not equal to the privilege of living for it.'

Archibald McIndoe, 1944[1]

'We don't live alone. We are members of one body. We are responsible for each other. And I tell you that the time will come when, if men will not learn that lesson, then they will be taught it in fire and blood and anguish.'

J.B. Priestley, 1945[2]

When aircrews piled into Lancasters and Wellingtons night after night and raid after raid, they did so against a background of unprecedented public awareness and engagement with their activity. This engagement with the bombers' war was far more than just registering the sound and vision of aircraft overhead on their way to battle. The RAF was a significant part of cultural and social life in Britain during the war, and public understanding went far beyond the often simplistic propaganda that had been the norm for the nation's armed forces before 1940.

Portrayals of the new air warriors, whether generated directly by the RAF or from non-official sources, spared few details of the reality of the combat environment. From 1940, emphasis was placed on the responsibility assumed by the bomber crews for the prosecution of the war, and the endurance such responsibility demanded of them – endurance which in itself generated a new kind of heroism. This was not simply a question of public presentation: this new definition of heroism came from within the RAF. Thus the Bomber Command Victoria Crosses were almost all awarded, not for the successful destruction of targets, but to men who shepherded home wounded aircraft, or put out fires, or who rescued colleagues. Even Guy Gibson, who participated in the most famous Bomber Command operation against the German dams of the Ruhr valley, was awarded his VC for circling the target after dropping his bouncing bomb to draw fire from the other aircraft in the squadron making their runs, rather than for the overall success of the raid.

Official efforts to build a relationship between the men of Bomber Command and the civilian population had begun almost from the outset of the war and the beginning of the offensive. In 1941 the Air Ministry published its first photographic record of the men and aircraft of Bomber Command. The text restated the RAF's conviction that, once it had enough bombers:

'... nothing could prevent the achievement of air supremacy and therefore of victory... These aircraft are to deliver that overwhelming onslaught which will bring the enemy to his knees and then lay him prostrate in the dust of his own cities.'[3]

Having outlined this most modern of strategic aims, the text went on to associate the men in the aircraft with far older historical role models:

'They are of the same breed as the men who each evening notched their dragon prows into the sun's red rim on the first voyage to Labrador, who braced the yards of the *Golden Hind* to round Cape Horn and who stumbled with Scott from the South Pole. "These twentieth century gentlemen of the shade, minions of the moon".'[4]

The text also took pains to ensure that the men of the bomber crews received as much attention as their more celebrated colleagues in Hurricanes and Spitfires:

'Bomber Command's pilots do not trace at vast speed fantastic patterns in the sky as did their comrades of Fighter Command when the Battle of Britain was won. They plod steadily on... to the abodes of the guilty.'[5]

As well as a constant stream of briefings to the news media from the Air Ministry and the RAF public relations department, there were broadcasts by Squadron Leader John Strachey (a former communist, air raid warden and PR officer to the Assistant Chief of the Air Staff). Strachey became a national figure as he relayed nightly to the nation the courage and sacrifice of the bomber crews. Then between 16 and 18 January 1943, journalists and foreign correspondents were allowed to participate directly in operational flights for the first time – and to take their readers and listeners with them. Flying with No. 5 Group, a selection of carefully chosen journalists, including Richard Dimbleby with Guy Gibson in 106 Squadron, saw Bomber Command carry out its first raid on Berlin for 14 months. The raid set many precedents: it was the first use of an all 4-engined bombing force, and the first use of target indicators (coloured incendiaries) by the Pathfinder Force. Casualties were light on the first night (1 Lancaster) but heavier on the second (19 Lancasters and 3 Halifaxes). The results of the bombing were disappointing but press coverage from participating journalists was certainly not. The RAF's Director of Public Relations reported that, 'the crews have been praised in a more outstanding way than ever before.'[6] Constraints were placed on the content of journalists' reports (they were not allowed to refer to the Pathfinder squadron, for instance) but otherwise it appears no direction as to the tone of such reports was given. The broadcasts that resulted from these operational flights brought the British public even closer to the men and machines of the strategic air offensive. For the substantial proportion of the civilian population living along the length of the eastern shorelines, the raids must have been very real indeed, as they would hear the aircraft leave, and know from the numbers returning if the night had gone well.

Press participation in operational flights continued until the end of the war, and enthusiasm by all parties for such participation was not diminished even when it proved to be as dangerous for the journalists as it could be for the crews. Indeed the narrow escapes and even the death of colleagues appeared to make for copy that was as acceptable to the RAF as it was gripping for the public. On 2 December 1943, four allied reporters, Ed Murrow, Lowell Bennett, Nordahl Greig and Norman Stockton were sent with 460 Squadron on a raid on Berlin. Previous raids had been successful but on that night the weather was very poor, breaking up the bomber stream before it reached the city. The Pathfinders failed to identify the relevant targets so the effect of the raid was negligible, and the patchy cloud cover allowed German night fighters to attack

SMILING THROUGH ... *By LEE*

[No. 2,611] NEWS AND PICTURES

"First it was reporters. Now it's Official Artists."

at full tilt the bedraggled bomber force struggling to get home. Forty air-craft were lost out of 458, with the loss of 228 men, including Greig and Stockton. Murrow, who made it back to London safely, made one of his most memorable broadcasts about his narrow escape on bomber D-for-Dog, and the courage of the crew who brought him home. His conclusions were made with what was by now the characteristic restraint and frankness about the reality of the bombers' war:

'It isn't a pleasant kind of war, the men doing it speak of it as a job. Yesterday afternoon, when the tapes were stretched out on the big map all the way to Berlin and back again, a young pilot with old eyes said to me, "I see we are working again tonight." That's the frame of mind in which the job is being done. The job isn't pleasant: it's terribly tiring. Men die in the sky while others are roasted alive in their cellars. Berlin last night wasn't a pretty sight. In about thirty-five minutes it was hit with about three times the amount of stuff that ever came down on London in a night long blitz. This is a calculated, remorseless campaign of destruction. Right now the mechanics are probably working on D-Dog, getting him ready to fly again.'[7]

Public support for the men and machines of the strategic air offensive went further than the attention and approval given to their war; the men and women of the Home Front were also prepared to make financial sacrifices for the campaign. The 1943 Wings for Victory fundraising drive was the most successful of the entire war.[8]

As always the campaign was heralded by thousands of posters all over the country urging the population to get involved. What is particularly notable about these posters is that the vast majority of them do not feature Spitfires (assumed in the post-war period to be 'the people's plane') but bomber aircraft. One popular image, appearing in a range of advertisements from the Wings for Victory effort to an ICI campaign, showed a composed Lancaster pilot looking down at the burning target he has just successfully destroyed.[9] In addition to these visual stimuli, Chancellor of the Exechequer Sir Kingsley Wood toured the country, reminding the citizens of the Home Front of their continuing debt:

'Even now we cannot measure all we owe to the Royal Air Force... the Royal Air Force have not been content to rest on their laurels. Every day, every hour and minute of the war, they have increased their effort and multiplied their blows on the enemy, making full use of every new bomb and every new 'plane. Bomber Command, Fighter Command, Coastal Command, Army Co-operation Command, each has added to the weight of the attack on the enemy. Now we are on the offensive and the Air Force is the spirit of that offensive.'[10]

From the *Daily Sketch*

The Chancellor had been scheduled to give just such a speech on his tour in Aberdeen, but a direct attack on the Scottish city three days before his arrival gave him cause to rewrite his words, and to remind the citizenry of their very direct contribution and participation in the strategic offensive:

'I know that one special motive will be behind your effort – you are determined to give the Royal Air Force all the backing at your command for so you will take vengeance on the enemy for the assault he has made on you… [I know] that you will not rest content with shewing courage when under attack. You will hit back. Those who can, bear arms in the field of battle, but for those whose place is at home, there is no better way of bringing the war home to the enemy than to hit back with war savings.'

Driven by such exhortations, and by their close relationship to the aircraft they heard above their homes every day, the public raised £507 million, over a million more than had been found for the previous Warships for Victory campaign.

All representations of the air war, whether produced by official or unofficial sources, were extremely popular. In 1945, a British Council review of culture entitled *Since 1939* noted:

'From first to last, however, it was the war in the air that captured the imagination of writer and reader alike. It was the one enthralling aspect of operational warfare which the civilian noncombatant could see for himself and in which he could feel himself to be deeply implicated. The fantastic air battles over the approaches to London during the "Battle of Britain" and the siren-heralded air raids were, in the long run, less impressive in this sense than the constant and visible reminder of the country's air potential on the great airfields up and down the land; in the ubiquitous aircrews; and in the moving sight and sound of the squadrons and wings of Bomber Command climbing through the failing light towards their objectives on the continent of Europe.'[11]

Rather than be diverted from the war outside their windows, the public could not get enough of plays, films, and writing about the men

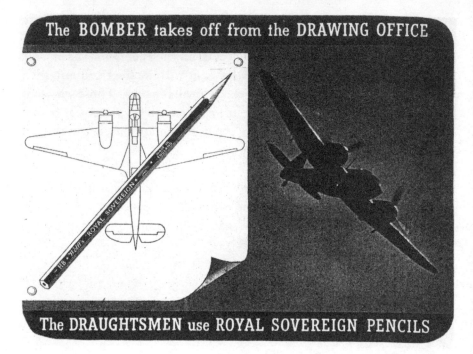

The BOMBER takes off from the DRAWING OFFICE

The DRAUGHTSMEN use ROYAL SOVEREIGN PENCILS

and operations of the RAF. Images of bombers were used to advertise everything from pencils to ICI's new armoured glass. Noel Coward's poem 'Lie in the Dark and Listen' was a typically popular piece with both civilians and aircrew (the poem was regularly reprinted in the magazine of the Guinea Pig Club).

> Lie in the dark and listen.
> It's clear tonight, so they're flying high,
> Hundreds of them, thousands perhaps,
> Riding the icy, moonlit sky.
> Men, material, bombs and maps,
> Altimeters and guns and charts,
> Coffee, sandwiches, fleece-lined boots,
> Bones and muscles and minds and hearts.
> English saplings with English roots
> Deep in the earth they have left below...
> Theirs is a world we can never know,
> Lie in the dark and listen.[12]

In the cinema, Michael Powell and Emeric Pressburger presented a particularly positive view of bomber crewmanship in their 1942 film *One of Our Aircraft is Missing*. The plot was centred around a Wellington crew who go on the run in occupied Holland after their aircraft crashes in a spectacularly unrepresentative fashion, without flames, smoke or injury, and allowing all crew members to exit the aircraft unscathed and in plenty of time. Through a combination of democratic teamwork, plucky Dutch resistance, and German stupidity, the crew make it back to England intact and ready for a new aircraft and a new mission. The film is notable for the reinforcement given to the bomber campaign by those in its path. Whilst hiding the crew, the Dutch resistance leader, played by Googie Withers, draws their attention to the bombers flying overhead:

'You see this – that's what you're doing for us – can you hear them running for shelter – can you understand what that means to all the occupied countries? To enslaved people having it drummed into their ears that the Germans are masters of the earth – seeing those masters running for shelter, seeing them crouching under tables… and hearing their steady hum night after night; that noise which is oil for the burning fires in our hearts.'

It is often forgotten that the lead character in Powell and Pressburger's masterpiece, *A Matter of Life and Death*, was from Bomber Command. Peter Carter, played by David Niven, is a master bomber on a Lancaster and veteran of 67 missions who should have died jumping from his burning aircraft but is missed by the angel sent to collect him. Carter is forced to appeal to stay on Earth in a enormous celestial courtroom. The producers (who also produced *The Life and Death of Colonel Blimp*) were not afraid to be critical of the conduct of the war, yet their portrayal of the men of the air offensive is entirely heroic and very much in the tradition of classical English drama – and we learn from the film that Heaven has a special section for aircrew that was full of the men from the bombers.

Audiences were even enthusiastic for theatrical representations. Terence Rattigan's play *Flare Path* was completed in 1941 but not staged until 1942 when the producers finally realised that there was commercial potential in such subject matter. Rattigan's story of one night's events at a bomber base in Lincolnshire (during a raid described by one character as 'a proper muck up from beginning to end') had a glittering premiere in the

West End, full of RAF top brass, including Charles Portal, who summoned Rattigan to his box to congratulate him personally. The production played to enthusiastic audiences and critics alike for 700 performances, and it is somewhat remarkable to think of the members of this audience hurrying past bomb debris and shelters to get to a theatre in the West End of London and spend two hours watching a play about a bombing raid.[13]

Only in the early years of the 21st century have tales of the bomber crews returned to the London stage. *Immortal* tells the story of the crew of a crashed Lancaster, hiding out in occupied Holland and trying to save the life of one of their number who is gravely injured. The play's writer, Ciaran McConville, had originally intended to write a comedy based on Bomber Command stereotypes, but as he researched the story and discovered the reality of life for the men of the Lancasters, he turned it into a drama instead. Working with RAF veterans and historians at the Imperial War Museum, McConville produced a movingly accurate reading of the dynamics of comradeship inside and outside the dying bomber aircraft. The crew is shown as a meritocratic whole, class and educational differences subordinate to each man's technical expertise within the command structure. And, above all, there is the urgent, consuming obligation felt by each one to ensure the survival of their wounded comrade. As one character says when urged by a Dutch resistance member to leave the casualty behind:

> 'Do you know who that is on the table? That hero, with his guts spilling over? That man who breathes and bleeds and flies through a nightly shower of hot metal? How can you know? How can you know that I can't let him go? Or how much it hurts me just to look at his face because where he's going I can't go with him?'[14]

Immortal was performed at the Edinburgh Festival and then, due to popular demand, made two separate transfers to London. What makes *Immortal* special, both dramatically and historically, is its close affinity with Powell and Pressburger's masterpiece, *A Matter of Life and Death*, written about the same men in the same war, but 60 years before. Both works are not shy of using rich, poetic language to describe the most modern and technologised of wars – McConville's descriptions are particularly insightful as he had no direct experience comparable to that of Powell and Pressburger. Here is the injured crewman in *Immortal* remembering his experience of a raid on Hamburg:

'It's a clear night, the moon splintering off the glass, and beneath us the clouds seem almost magical, breaking away into strands, the ground black like a pool of water. And there she is ahead of us. It is so beautiful. A smudge of flames against a mighty tower of soot and fumes. And the tracers come floating up to meet us. Blues and reds and yellows. So slow you think you could just move out of the way of them. And all around us the Bombers are falling out of the sky. Blue searchlights snap on to them first, the bright white manual lights following suit. And then the momentary wait for the hail of hot metal to hit their underbellies. Two or three at a time they burn, disintegrating as they fall, until they are just empty iron crosses. We hear one crew screaming on the radio. But up *here* it's all just music. The smack of the flak on the fuselage. It's almost rhythmical. A heartbeat. If this is it, I'm going to go happy. I'm going with my boys. I'm dancing...'[15]

The strongest continuity between the two works is that the supernatural is at the heart of their drama. In *A Matter of Life and Death*, the master bomber of a Lancaster pleads to be allowed to stay on earth before a celestial courtroom. In *Immortal*, one or more of the crewmen may already have perished, pulled back across the divide between life and death by the bounds of comradeship and the overriding need to save the life of one of their own. Both works therefore share the assumptions that the men of Bomber Command are worthy not only of divine intervention but that their stories can be told using the language and dramatic devices of classical theatre.

One significant cultural intervention during the war by the RAF had particular resonance for the work of Archibald McIndoe and his patients at East Grinstead. McIndoe was not the only consultant to the RAF engaged in the work of making the faces of their aircrew; at almost the same time as McIndoe began his work, the RAF selected Eric Kennington to be its official portrait artist and and commissioned from him a series of 150 portraits of serving aircrew. Kennington had already achieved a considerable reputation as a portraitist and war artist in the First World War for works such as *The Kensingtons at Laventie* and had completed two series of portraits at the behest of the Army (the Arab series and the Infantry series) in the Second World War. His subjects included Chief of the Air Staff Charles Portal (who commented that Kennington portraits gave their subjects rather a lot to live up to), fighter aces 'Sailor' Malan, 'Ginger' Lacey and Douglas Bader, Air Raid Warden Jones and various airmen from occupied nations who went unnamed. The series was completed by 1942 and shown in both the (British) National Gallery and the Museum of Modern Art in New York to great public acclaim (Kennington included two portraits of members of the Eagle Squadron for the American exhibition). Some pictures were made into postcards but the success of the series was such that the RAF had a hardback edition made, *Drawing the RAF*, in which each portrait had an accompanying biography of its subject, including service records and citations. Group Captain Helmore, author and broadcaster on RAF subjects, included several of these portraits in his *Air Commentary* (Helmore also wrote as 'Flight Commander' during the First World War – see quotation on page 23):

'To you I can only offer the masterpiece portraits of Eric Kennington, some memory of the great fighters of the air whose deeds have made a mockery of words and in whose faces can be found something of that inner radiance which may yet raise man above the level of the beasts that perish.'[16]

Despite such whole-hearted endorsement, Kennington found his time with the RAF to be as stressful as it was rewarding. Whilst he was as comfortable with aircrew as he had been with the Kensingtons in the First World War, he found it hard to come to terms with the fact that many of his subjects were killed before their portraits were finished. In the autumn of 1942 he resigned his position as official war artist to the RAF and received the following testimonial from the service:

> 'You have given the Nation, and through them the RAF, a unique collection of their most celebrated personnel which... will have an increasing historical and traditional value as the years go on.'[17]

However hard the experience had been for Kennington he had indeed provided the RAF with some instant tradition, bringing it into line with the older services which had been commissioning status-enhancing portraits of their officers for generations. And he had provided the RAF with a human face for it to present to the public – which makes it all the more remarkable that, ultimately, the RAF was as happy to have the public know and understand the faces made by Archibald McIndoe as they did those of Eric Kennington. Indeed, the two men were linked by one man, Richard Hillary, who was a patient of McIndoe's at East Grinstead and who sat for Kennington. The artist had been introduced to Hillary by T.E. Lawrence after both of them had been impressed by *The Last Enemy*. After Hillary's premature death in a training accident, Kennington completed the portrait for Hillary's mother; in it can be seen all too clearly the effects of fire on perishable flesh. Of all the Kennington portraits of RAF crew, it is this portrait, and a companion one of McIndoe by Anna Zinkeisen, which hang today in the National Portrait Gallery.

If the work of Eric Kennington was to construct the face of the RAF airman for the public, then Archibald McIndoe's lot was to reconstruct it. McIndoe and Kennington were, in effect, two sides of the same coin with which the RAF attempted to obtain public understanding of, and assent to, its vision of the new war and its warriors. But, from the outset, Kennington's work was intended for public display in a way that severely burned patients were not. The process of integrating the facially disfigured into a variety of public contexts was not just a complex mixture of medical and military imperatives, it was, above all, a matter of human

understanding and instinct. Nothing was more important or more difficult to manage than human instinct; the instinctive reaction to a severely
disrupted human face is to be repelled, to turn away, to ignore. And it is
in dealing with the matter of human instinct that the presence of
Archibald McIndoe was crucial, for it was he who persuaded the public
to turn back, to look his patients in the face, and then to begin the
process of understanding what such men represented.

The question of relations between the severely burned patient group
and their local, professional and national environments was an issue that
needed to be resolved within months of the first 'burned boy' being
received at East Grinstead. The location of the unit, in the centre of a
small prosperous town 40 miles outside London, posed unique problems
for McIndoe. Not only was he faced with, as he himself put it, 'the opportunity of surgically restoring a large consecutive series of facial burns in
which destruction has been massive', and for which existing treatment
methods were patently unsuitable – indeed even dangerous – he also had
to resolve the situation in public.[18] His patients who manifested such
massive destruction were highly exposed at East Grinstead – contact
with the townsfolk could not be avoided – and relations between the two
parties required careful negotiation. Yet McIndoe's management of
those relations, and of the relations between RAF casualties and the
service itself, was far more than a question of mutual accustomisation.
He determined that the social environment in which the medical treatment took place was a crucial factor in the success of the repair. He
therefore actively sought the participation of the public and the service
in the treatment process, over and above securing their acceptance of the
casualties among them.

McIndoe's burned airmen were no ordinary patients; at first they were
'the few', the knights of the air, to whom so much was owed by so many.
They were young and energetic, many with life styles and sports cars that
matched their dashing reputation. Above all, once first aid and primary
care had been administered, they were not bed-bound. Very many of
Ward III's patients had suffered only the external trauma of burning, and
had few or no internal or orthopaedic injuries which would impair their
mobility. The situation was the same regardless of the stage their reconstructive surgical schedule had reached – indeed patients mid-schedule
could be even more challenging to the public gaze than those with only
burns trauma, a situation McIndoe well appreciated:

'... the immediate results are often more horrifying than the original condition until the resolving influence of time has softened their asperities and enabled movement, expression and texture to return.'[19]

Such patients might have patchwork faces, or the trunk-like tube pedicles from face to shoulder to graft a new nose or ear, but they could still walk, drive, drink and dance. Their boredom threshold was non-existent and, if they could not return to flying immediately, they wanted to return to a normal life and living environment as soon as possible. The very shortest of walks out of the hospital took them to East Grinstead, where could be found pubs, restaurants, a dance hall and cinemas.

Before civilians could contribute to the reconstruction process, both patient and public had to get used to each other. This meant getting the public into the hospital and the patients to resume their lives as comfortably as possible in public. Although this process has not been formally recorded, it appears that McIndoe himself addressed local worthies, hosted seminars and lectures at the hospital, and arranged concerts and sporting events in its grounds. He prevailed upon the ladies of the larger houses in the town to visit the ward and its patients, to provide fresh flowers on a weekly basis, and to act as his ambassadors for East Grinstead's population at large. The entire staff of the hospital were committed to this process. After their long shifts, East Grinstead nurses, many of them local, visited townsfolk to explain the medical work and its physical consequences, and to seek their co-operation and invitations for the patients into their houses.

A fair amount of initiative was taken by the citizens of East Grinstead themselves. Mabel Osbourne was a young waitress at the Whitehall restaurant when the first group of burn patients entered the restaurant. She nervously served them and, at closing time, joined a meeting of her fellow staff to discuss how they should handle such customers. Mabel remembered:

'We sort of made up our minds about what we should do. [We thought] Oh let's look at them – look them full in the eyes and just see them, and treat them as if we don't see it. We'll look at them and not look away from them and speak to them. And that's what we did... and we got so used to it we never took any notice after that.'[20]

Other townspeople handled their introductions to McIndoe's patients slightly differently from Mabel and her workmates. For a recent television documentary, Stella Clapton remembered her husband turning sternly to her as they were about to enter the Whitehall saying, 'Don't you bat an eyelid when you go in, not an eyelid.'[21] Mabel and the Claptons were among the first townspeople to experience both the look and the practical hindrances of burn injuries, as described by Bill Simpson in his memoir, *The Way of Recovery*:

'... those first sorties into the world outside the hospital were painful, especially for the youngest amongst us. Without hands, for instance, it was impossible to do anything without assistance. It was embarrassing to have someone pouring beer down your throat, wiping your mouth, blowing your nose, handling your money. It was even more embarrassing to have to make for the gentleman's cloakroom in pairs. Naturally no young man experienced such a loss of his independence without resenting it strongly, for it made him as helpless as a small child and robbed him of all his dignity.'[22]

In particular, the resolution of Mabel and her friends regarding their new group of customers had such a positive effect that the Whitehall restaurant became an unofficial hospital social club, while the manager, Bill Gardner, became an unofficial member of the hospital welfare team:

'Bill... took a special personal interest in our welfare. At the bar he would stand and drink with us, but he always had one eye on those of us who tended to drink too much. He contributed very largely to our happiness while we were in the neighbourhood. Whenever we felt particularly conscious of being ugly and deformed, we always knew there was a welcome waiting for us at Bill's, and that he would soon laugh away any tendency we had towards gloom or depression.'[23]

The first edition of *The Guinea Pig* magazine (April 1944) also paid its own tribute to Gardner's care:

'Guinea Pigs are notorious for their nocturnal habits. They are a constant source of worry to Bill the Gardner who has to keep on supplying them with their staple diet. Fortunately he understands their ways and caters from their need for 'Light' [ale] refreshment. If you are the wheel-chair type he helps you walk the plank; if you do a line with the odd nurse he finds a table not too much in the public eye; and he has a special way of dealing with Guinea Pigs with troublesome tails. How often do we Guinea Pigs recall going down the Gardner Path to Guinea Pig Hall?'[24]

The Whitehall was part of a large entertainment complex in the centre of town which included a cinema and the Rainbow ballroom. Rather than discourage this strange and expanding customer group, the owners of the complex, Letheby & Christopher, followed the example set by their staff, and made McIndoe's patients welcome. There were always seats in the cinema reserved for them and standing invitations to the weekly dances at the Rainbow. The Whitehall was Ward III's outpost in the town, and when 'a line with a nurse' led to the altar, as it did with increasing frequency in East Grinstead and at the other RAF burns units, it hosted the wedding receptions. A report in the *East Grinstead Gazette* on one such union demonstrated how, for the townspeople, accommodation became affection, when 'Hoke' Mahn married a local nurse. Their story, with a large accompanying picture, was front page news, and a large crowd gathered outside the church to cheer when the happy couple appeared.[25] Wedding photographs were an extremely popular newspaper item – the *Evening Standard* of 1942 has a picture of a newly-married couple, preferably from the services, nearly every day – so the Mahns were East Grinstead's very own version.

McIndoe's demands on East Grinstead were also practical. As well as providing everything from fresh garden flowers for Ward III to library books, he also asked that patients be received as guests and more by local families. Family houses with rooms to spare became unofficial convalescent homes. Kathleen and Johnny Dewar, of the whisky manufacturing family, turned over their country house to McIndoe, and their convalescent guests included Bill Simpson, Richard Hillary and Colin Hodgkinson. Kathleen Dewar encouraged both Simpson and Hillary to write memoirs of their experiences. Simpson remembered this of the period:

'Many houses were thrown open to us. In them we were never allowed to feel in any way peculiar. We were treated as members of the family,

Gentlemen of the Guinea Pig Club arrive at the Whitehall for the Dinner

and from the contacts we made friendships grew which are unlikely ever to be broken.'[26]

And it was not just those East Grinstead families with rooms or houses to spare who threw them open to McIndoe's patients and their families. When rear gunner John Bubb was wounded in 1941, he spent six months having his jaw reconstructed in Ward III. His wife Betty visited him every weekend for the duration of his treatment, staying with a local family who moved their son out of his own room so she could sleep comfortably. Betty remembered their kindness in helping her through what must have been the ordeal of John's reconstruction, and in particular remembered her hostess' excellent cooking for Sunday lunch, for which she would take no money or food coupons from her guest for the entire period.[27]

As the burned RAF aircrew moved around East Grinstead, their acceptance into the community answered McIndoe's challenge to the town to be a part of the therapeutic environment. East Grinstead provided an initial first step between hospital ward and public life, easing the re-entry of the facially disfigured into society. The town had become a part of the medical team at the hospital. Accommodation became encouragement, affection and communal pride in what was perceived as the town's unique contribution to the war effort. So successful was the relationship between town, hospital and patient group that patients were actively discouraged from going home to their families too early, and encouraged to remain in the therapeutic community which had been created. George Morley described the reasons for this in an RAF pamphlet on plastic surgery written after the war:

'... Mental and moral rehabilitation demands serious consideration from the very instant that these patients commence treatment in the Centre... It is not usually advantageous to return these patients prematurely to their homes, unless they have domestic anxieties which they can alleviate, because the sympathy which they may receive may be misdirected and discouraging. It is usually more beneficial to proceed to active rehabilitation and to set the patient well on the road to full recovery, after which he should certainly return to his family for a period. The idea here is to return him home when he is full of pride in his prowess, inclined to mix with his fellows and to show off his abilities, rather than prematurely to send him into an environment of sympathy instead of encouragement.'[28]

The contribution of the town was also acknowledged in the memoirs of the patients themselves. Simpson's work recalled:

'Here in this southern town there was never any suggestion that disfigurement should be concealed, and that the disfigured should be confined to hospital... quite the contrary. Inspired by Archibald

Squadron Leader W. Simpson

McIndoe himself, we were encouraged to circulate freely, no matter how bad our physical condition appeared, and the result was a complete success. I can only look back with horror at the examples that I had seen elsewhere in the past of attempts to conceal the disfigured. Here in this southern town, morale was kept high.'[29]

Evidence of the town's pride in such tributes may be found in an edition of the *East Grinstead Gazette* which carried a prominent advertisement for the local bookshop, Edwin Tooth Ltd, announcing that, '*The Way of Recovery* by Squadron Leader W. Simpson DSO is now in stock.'[30]

This was Simpson's second book about his injury and featured prominently a photograph of his injured self, in his RAF uniform.

In return for its commitment to the patients, East Grinstead gained national attention not only for the efforts of the doctors and patients in its midst, but also for its own efforts in bringing about successful recoveries. The 'small southern town' became famous, especially after the publication of several patient memoirs from 1941, and became known, to its considerable pride, as 'the town that didn't stare'. The first article to note this national exposure appeared in the local paper in August 1941:

'The fact that the Maxillo-Facial Unit had been attached to the hospital had created great interest throughout the country and a number of distinguished personalities had visited the hospital. It was, in fact, the most important unit of its kind in the country and its fame was spreading not only throughout this country but throughout the world.'[31]

From then on, all articles about the hospital, Ward III and its patients were carried prominently on the front page. Special emphasis was placed on the advanced nature of both the medical work and the equipment – coverage was given to the 'latest type of anaesthetic apparatus' installed in the operating theatres by Sir Ivan Magill, and the research efforts of the various specialists were recorded and praised.[32] When the hospital's name was changed from 'Cottage Hospital' to 'Queen Victoria Hospital', the newspaper mourned the loss of the local connection but reminded its readers that the new name better befitted 'a hospital of international fame.'[33] Regular features kept the townspeople up to date with normal operations at the hospital ('this week we tell of the wonderful activities of the surgical department'[34]).

Each Christmas edition featured an article on how the holiday was spent at the hospital – indeed the social life of the hospital was of very particular interest to the town as many of the country's most popular entertainers came down to perform and visit the by-now-famous Ward III. A thrilled *Gazette* painstakingly listed the visiting celebrities and, 'distinguished artists [who] have at considerable personal sacrifice given Sunday afternoon performances', including Flanagan and Allen, Tommy Trinder, Joyce Grenfell, Douglas Byng and Frances Day.[35] The last, star of the racy 1936 comedy, *The Girl from Maxim's*, was a particular favourite of the Guinea Pigs, especially when she sang a specially amended version of Cole

Porter's 'Let's Do It' which included the lines 'The boys do it... Even Archie McIndoe does it... '[36] She became a regular feature of the hospital's entertainment programme, and continued her involvement with the Guinea Pig Club well after the war. (After the arrival of the US forces in preparation for D-Day, their stars also visited the hospital, including Clark Gable, whose arrival created even more excitement than that of visiting politicians or royalty.) Much advantage was taken of McIndoe's prewar connections which had brought him into close (surgical) contact with professionals most concerned with their photographic image and its perfection. McIndoe's biographer noted that, 'the *McIndoe Nose* was beginning to be talked about [in the early 1930s]'.[37] The combination of McIndoe's connections, his considerable personal charisma, and the fame of the hospital's work proved irresistible for many of Britain's wartime stars.

It was not just entertainers whose presence in the town caused such pride. In 1943 the *Gazette* noted the fame of the town in official and military circles, recording visits to the hospital by Harold Balfour, Clement Attlee, Harold Nicolson, and William Astor. Under the headline, 'A Year of Great Achievement – World Wide Reputation', it was noted that:

'In the *Wings for Victory* campaign, Lord Kindersley [Chairman of the hospital and President of the National Savings Committee] had met airmen of all ranks and there was not one who did not recognise the grand work that was being done... [the hospital's] work and the work of their splendid staff was known throughout the world.'[38]

The newspaper also recognised and publicised its readers' own contribution to this 'grand work', praising:

'The unselfish help and genuine interest of the community in which the hospital is placed... so many have contributed so much to making what could be a depressing experience into a period to look back upon with something akin to pleasure.'[39]

After 1942 local interest and pride in the hospital was attracting national attention. Evidence of this is given in an article in the *Reader's Digest* from November 1943, written after the town had suffered heavy casualties from a bomb hitting the cinema (108 dead, 235 injured):

'East Grinstead in Sussex, England, is a town with a broken heart and a heart breaking job… Conditioned by their own heartbreak, these townspeople know how to do their unparallelled job making the horribly burned RAF boys from nearby Queen Victoria Hospital know they can still live in society. These lads with the shapeless raw, red faces come down to the town each day. They don't want to come at first. They walk down the street, trying not to see themselves in shop windows, their curled and sometimes fingerless hands in their pockets. Their faces are not of this world during the long period of skin grafting. Often the nose or both the ears are gone. Their eyes are tiny, bleak, glistening marbles, and the look in them is not one to write about.

The first time you see one of these boys the blood goes out of your face and your stomach rocks. You curse yourself but you can't help it. But the good people of East Grinstead stop these chaps in the street and chat with them. They take them into their homes and give them tea. The girls invite them to dances. And not even the children stare at them. One obvious shudder might undo weeks of excruciating work at the QVH. So in East Grinstead the most ghastly burned boy is the most welcome. His face is the job of the hospital, but his will to live is a job that is in the hands of the townsfolk.'[40]

East Grinstead had risen to Archibald McIndoe's challenge to become a part of the therapeutic team dealing with the problem of the burned airman. In doing so it provided him with evidence that the social environment in which surgical reconstruction took place was as important as the medical environment. Success in the immediate geographical environment of East Grinstead was only half the battle. When the patients walked in the town's high street it was as RAF aircrew, and it was the context and environment of the Royal Air Force which was just as important a factor in recovery as the social environment of the town. Comments of townspeople, such as Don Armstrong, bore out this conviction. Armstrong was a boy when the war brought the burned aircrew to the town and told how:

'We as kids were very aware that they were heroes. We'd watched the Battle of Britain. We'd watched these guys operating over our heads and we had a very great affection for them.'[41]

So McIndoe's challenge was made not just to East Grinstead but also to the RAF. His patients needed to be made to feel as secure in their chosen service environment as they did in their immediate social lives. McIndoe's attention had been drawn to the figure of the disabled service-man long before his involvement with East Grinstead – indeed before he had even specialised in plastics. McIndoe arrived in Depression-hit London in 1931 from the Mayo Clinic in the United States where he had trained as an abdominal surgeon. A fellow student and friend, Julian Brunner, who came to London soon after, remembered that they had both been struck by the numbers of injured First World War veterans begging on street corners – McIndoe had been particularly affected by veterans playing cornets or selling matches in Piccadilly.[42] After he became involved directly with military casualties, the image of damaged men begging, busking or selling matches strongly motivated his dealings with both civilian and service authorities. He was determined that it should not happen to his patients and was convinced that insecurity about the future was a factor in patient recovery, and therefore, 'this requires the personal attention of the surgeon'.[43]

McIndoe's first exchange with the Royal Air Force in the matter of its dealings with its casualties came over the issue of uniform. Air Ministry Regulation A.310 restated in May 1940 that, 'it is a general rule that Officers not serving on the active list of the RAF... shall not wear uniform.'[44] Instead personnel invalided from the service could wear the King's Badge – 'an outward and visible sign that the wearer has served his country' – and a sign often present on the battered lapels of many of the cornet-playing veterans of the Great War.[45] Convalescent but still serving personnel could wear 'convalescent blues' a crude approxima tion of battledress in calico, more akin to the prison yard than the hospital ward. The patients of East Grinstead fell between these two categories: on the one hand many of them could expect to see active service again after or during their reconstructive treatment; on the other, the periods in between active service and surgery could be sufficiently long as to necessitate invaliding from the service.

The original consignment of convalescent blues that was sent to East Grinstead was ignored, and like their counterparts on active service, McIndoe's patients wore battledress 'on all occasions'. Although no correspondence with the Air Ministry appears to have been generated, 'the question [of uniforms] emanated from Mr McIndoe's hospital at

East Grinstead' via Harold Whittingham, Director General of the RAFMS.[46] In December 1941 the formality of amending the regulations took place:

'Authority is given for officers and airmen who have been invalided from the RAF on account of wounds or other injuries attributable to war service to continue to wear their appropriate uniforms as long as they remain patients under treatment in the hospital in which they were being treated at the time of the invaliding.'[47]

The amendment only covered RAF aircrew, and it was not without opposition from the civil servants at the Air Ministry. In a minute against the amendment, one declared that, 'in any case the surgeon in charge is not in my view the competent person to authorise [the change of regulation].'[48] The minute is thus notable as it is the first and last time anyone at the Air Ministry ever questioned the competence of Archibald McIndoe.

The importance of the wearing of battledress by severely injured aircrew cannot be underestimated. The first time a disfigured man walked down East Grinstead High Street, in the same uniform in which he fought and was injured, he changed the definition of 'casualty' in the RAF. Casualty no longer meant 'a gallant wounded soldier with his arm in a sling' or a discreet eye patch, it meant ordeal by fire.[49] It also meant that despite the horror and labour of disfigurement, the casualties were effectively still on active service – their participation in the war was ongoing. It was not just faces that were being reconstructed at East Grinstead, but the whole concept of heroism. For the casualties themselves, and their public, their role was clear:

'... they always knew that their disfigurement was not considered dishonourable. They realised, too that there was no cause for despair, and that by appearing in public, they were keeping the public aware of the realities of war.

It is true that in spite of eight years of world war within the last thirty, the men and women in this and other countries are peculiarly unprepared to witness and accept the marks that bear witness to the real horrors of war that are worn by their fellow beings. Our leaders have told us that, in their opinion, this war cannot be brought to a close without a considerable sacrifice of blood, and so the sooner we can accustom ourselves to the reality of war scars, the better it will be both for the unharmed and the wounded.'[50]

For its part, the RAF accepted these new definitions of casualty and active service. The new definitions of heroism and endurance that it had made for its servicemen accommodated those disfigured by their service. For the RAF, as well as the public, McIndoe's patients were still on active service, and the service's advocacy for such men was as energetic and forceful as it was for their uninjured crewmates. This was not window-dressing for the public but a deep sense of responsibility. The Chief of the Air Staff himself, Charles Portal, spelled out:

'... the moral reasons why we had a duty towards this particular class of personnel. There was no parallel in the Services to aircrew who fought the enemy with hundreds of gallons of petrol on board... the fire risk was greater than in any other arm of the Service apart from the Fleet Air Arm.'[51]

It is worth noting also that the RAF was clear that what it owed was as much to bomber crews as to The Few of the Battle of Britain – after all, 'hundreds of gallons of fuel' referred to bombers, not fighters.

In clearly stating its moral responsibilities for its injured servicemen, the RAF also offered reassurance to its uninjured aircrew:

'CAS [Chief of the Air Staff] suggested that the importance of the morale of aircrew placed them in a different category [from the other Services]. It was generally recognised that aircrew personnel were selected from the finest material and this was another reason for special treatment.'[52]

The service as a whole was highly aware of both the dangers of fire and of McIndoe's work with their burned crewmates, and this had become a matter of service morale. There was considerable pride in what was being done for these men but, conversely, should those efforts falter, morale would be adversely affected. The Air Ministry was keen to avoid the isolated incidents such as the one where convalescent aircrew had (wrongly) incurred:

THE RECONSTRUCTION OF WARRIORS

'... a hospital charge for maintenance. This discrimination affected adversely not only those against whom it was applied but the others undergoing treatment alongside them, and when the latter eventually went back to duty the news of what was happening was spread around the Service with harmful effects.'[53]

Portal emphasised the RAF's ready acceptance of its responsibilities in the matter, and his own preference for the service to look after its own, rather than rely on the state:

'The state has in any case to care for them until rehabilitated, so why not within the Service so as to maintain the highest possible morale as an aid to recovery and spare them the humiliation of being turned out simply because they have no future – i.e. are a bad military investment; most of all for the benefit of the morale of aircrew as a whole.'

His opinions were shared by the Under-Secretary of State for Air:

'It is an almost inevitable part of their Service that aircrew have constantly to contend not only against human enemies but also the risk of fire and the risk of a crash. The knowledge that, if they are seriously injured while flying on duty, their treatment will be in every way the best that can be provided both medically and otherwise, cannot fail to contribute to high morale in flying and air fighting.'[54]

Looking back, RAFMS surgeon David Matthews, one of the original four trained by McIndoe at East Grinstead, commented:

'The knowledge of the existence of McIndoe and all he stood for must have comforted many an airman in moments of apprehension in their dangerous lives. This imperishable contribution to victory in the darkest days of this country's history is his lasting memorial.'[55]

Matthews went on to become consultant plastic surgeon at the Great Ormond Street Hospital for Children.

The RAF had clearly considered all aspects of the effect on service morale McIndoe's patients might have. In response to a query about, 'the possible disturbing effects their association with other members of aircrew might have', the reply came that:

'It is considered that there is no evidence that the disfigurement resulting from burns has effected adversely the morale and the efficiency of other members of aircrews; in fact the general feeling is that aircrews are very pleased to serve with such stout-hearted individuals.

It is further considered that, if personnel who have suffered are relieved from active duties, their personal discomfort would be increased and they tend to develop an inferiority complex.'[56]

From statements such as these it was clear that the RAF had accepted not only its moral responsibility for its casualties but also McIndoe's convictions about the medical importance of connections to their environment. In December 1944 the Under-Secretary of State for Air wrote in a report to a War Cabinet committee that:

'To ensure the best possible care for the badly injured is not only a moral duty to men who have served us well; it is also a necessary element in good rehabilitation. The surgeons who treat the most seriously injured cases are agreed that high morale is of vital importance to recovery. No man, they say, should be allowed to doubt that his recovery will be complete or to fear the prospect of enduring disability in after-life. He must feel complete confidence in the treatment he is receiving and the certainty that nothing will be spared which might contribute to his full restoration.'[57]

Another Air Ministry correspondent spoke with the confidence of one who:

'... recently had the advantage of meeting Mr McIndoe [who] laid great stress on the psychological importance of encouraging the patient to have confidence in the ability of the surgeon to restore him to complete normality and claimed that the patient's attitude of mind has a great deal to do with the success of the treatment.'[58]

For hundreds of Guinea Pigs 'full restoration' meant a return to flying operations, often in the middle of their schedule of reconstruction. Tom

Gleave assumed command of RAF Manston in Kent, Richard Hillary returned to train on night bombers, Alan Morgan (despite losing eight fingers to frostbite) resumed his trade as a navigator. Roy Lane, burned in the Battle of Britain, was part of Orde Wingate's operations in Burma, supplying the Chindits by air until his capture and beheading by the Japanese. Geoffrey Page eventually rejoined a fighter unit flying support for the D-Day invasion. Others, although they could not fly combat operations, flew on as trainers or testers. This was not window-dressing. The RAF still had a pressing need for these highly trained operatives, even those whose flying days were over; if a patient could walk about East Grinstead, he could certainly put his operational experience and skills to use in an RAF control room. This necessity was emphasised by the RAFMS in June 1941:

'From the practical posting point of view, it is necessary to employ personnel, who are temporarily or permanently unfit for flying, in posts which require knowledge of operational flying. These posts, such as "operations rooms", "regional control", "sector control", "duty pilot", etc are mainly on operational stations. The policy is not to waste this class of personnel in Technical Training, Balloon or Maintenance Commands.'[59]

By 1942, when schemes were in place for skilled aircrew to work in Ministry of Aircraft Production (MAP) factories, McIndoe wrote to Air Marshal Babington of the MAP that:

'It should be borne in mind that by no means all the injured pilots go to MAP; for instance, Air Marshal Sir Sholto Douglas has personally selected suitable candidates for the position of Comptrollers in Operations Rooms, and obviously the necessities of the RAF must come before the requirements of the MAP.'[60]

Douglas' involvement is worth noting as it confirms the interest throughout the Air Council in McIndoe's patients. Both Sholto Douglas and Hugh Dowding (Commander in Chief of Fighter Command until the end of 1940) took particular care with this group of men, as their experience of the injury was very close to home. Both men appointed Robert Wright as their personal assistant (Dowding during the Battle of Britain until his retirement and Douglas thereafter), and both men also appointed him their official biographer after the war. Just before his death, Dowding wrote to Tom Gleave how he had:

'... always felt the Guinea Pigs close to my heart since their institution. They will stand as a moral of self-sacrificing service so long as their record remains in the pages of history.'[61]

Despite failing a medical in 1939 on the grounds of weak eyesight, Wright was eventually posted as a navigator to 604 Squadron (Beaufighters), then to 85 Squadron (Mosquitos). In 1944 Wright's engine failed during a night flying test and he was badly burned in the crash. He was taken first to the burns unit at Ely and then claimed by McIndoe on one of his fortnightly rounds, so qualifying for Guinea Pig Club membership. During a period of convalescence at his home in Kent, Wright's house was hit by a V2 and he had to return to East Grinstead for another set of repairs.[62]

Above all, it was the settling of the pension and invalidity arrangements for severely injured aircrew that showed most strongly the RAF's commitment to its burn casualties. Members of the Air Council and senior civilian officials of the Air Ministry were prepared to go to great lengths in taking on the Treasury as well as the other branches of the armed services to secure the financial and professional futures of McIndoe's patients. The main point of contention was the length of time a convalescing casualty was entitled to full pay and allowances before he had to return to active service or leave the RAF. This had originally been 90 days, and if the patient was not ready to return he was then invalided out of the service. This period was patently unsuitable for plastic surgery patients and the rule was quickly changed to six months. As the war went on, it became obvious that scrapping the 90-day rule in favour of six months was not going to be enough either; burns patients were going back and forth between operational positions and East Grinstead over a number of years, so new regulations would have to be put in place to take account of this exceptional time span for reconstruction.

In April 1943 the Treasury had proposed a new limit of 12 months with very special exceptions being entitled to 18 months, but was insistent that, 'a limit should be put on the time the RAF officers may be kept in full time pay beyond their sick leave entitlement.'[63] In August 1943 the Air Ministry turned the offer down, because, 'after very careful consideration it does not meet our case'.[64] Their counter-proposal for, 'aircrew personnel undergoing plastic surgical treatment for attributable disabilities', was that where the possibility existed, however far in the future, that the patient could return to duty, that they should, 'continue to receive full pay without time limit'. Accompanying this demand was a clear statement of the value placed on all its servicemen by the RAF:

> 'Our primary consideration in this matter is that we should conserve to the utmost what will probably be freely admitted to be the most valuable fighting personnel in the fighting service, namely aircrew personnel. To this end we are most anxious to avoid the loss of aircrew personnel through the arbitrary operations of the present rule which limits to 12 months, or in special cases to 18 months, entitlement of officers to full pay in cases of absence from duty on account of sickness or injury.'

The Treasury was horrified by the idea of unlimited paid sick leave and responded by proposing to raise the limit to 14 months but at the same time that the 18 month special exceptions provision be withdrawn on the grounds that only a few airmen would qualify for it.[65] The suggestion provoked immediate alarm in the Air Ministry; Folliott Sandford, Assistant Under-Secretary of State, took up the case, warning the Treasury of the consequences of its action in no uncertain terms:

> 'This matter of special sick leave for personnel undergoing plastic surgical treatment has attracted a good deal of attention here, and at least two Service Members of Council have shown considerable personal interest in it. If the suggestion in MacKay's letter is to be pressed, the matter will certainly have to go up to Air Council level here, and before submitting it I should like to be sure that the

Treasury really do wish to press the point. It seems to me that it would be a great mistake that the Treasury, having made a concession which has attracted a good deal of attention and which is accepted here as a very valuable one, should endeavour to withdraw it a few months later on the ground that the rate of aircrew casualties has recently been lower than expected. Quite apart from the effect on the individuals directly concerned, the withdrawal of the concession now would cause a great deal of irritation and annoyance not only in the Air Ministry, but among officers who have interested themselves in those unfortunate cases, and it does seem to me that insistence would give the Treasury a name for needlessly hard logic which they do not deserve. Moreover I cannot see what effective answer a Minister could give in the House if he were asked to state the reasons why a concession which was made as recently as December 1943, had been withdrawn in August 1944.'[66]

The issue was complicated by interventions from the Ministry of Pensions and the Admiralty who vigorously objected to special treatment for aircrew. Further complications were added by the increasing numbers of burn casualties injured during 1944 and the fact that the war was perceived to be in its final stages. Thus, in mid-argument, the issue became not about, 'conserving the most valuable fighting personnel in the fighting service', but about how aircrew wounded in war should be treated in peace.

Sandford was right in his predictions that members of the Air Council who had shown 'considerable personal interest' in the matter would become involved in the dispute. Charles Portal had become personally involved with East Grinstead in 1943 and he was proving himself to be a dedicated advocate on the patients' behalf. Over the next 18 months he proved immovable on his servicemen's right 'to remain in the Service as long as we had treatment to give them'.[67]

Despite a schedule so busy he rarely slept at home or for more than four hours a night, the Chief of the Air Staff always seems to have had time for McIndoe. They developed a close relationship (ignored by Portal's biographers) and must have made a formidable pair. Portal sought closely to associate his own commitment to the burn casualties with that of McIndoe, writing to the surgeon that, 'nothing could be too good for the men whose interests we have at heart'. During 1943 Portal and McIndoe began to correspond regularly, Portal helping McIndoe out in bringing pressure to bear on the Ministry of Health and Ministry of Works over a new hospital building. In November 1944 Portal was at the heart of the dispute between the RAF and the Treasury. He wrote to McIndoe that:

'I am inclined to continue to press for our full proposal which was that these men should remain on full pay until either "surgical finality" was reached or it was considered by the Medical Authorities to be in the individual's best interest that he should be invalided from the Service.

The fault... is that it leaves uncovered the worst cases which fortunately are also few. We should therefore remain vulnerable to our own consciences and to outside attack when for a very little extra money this could be avoided.

I am glad to tell you that the Secretary of State is prepared to go to the Chancellor of the Exchequer and plead for the acceptance of our full proposals. It would help him very much if I could show him a letter from you confirming what you told me on the telephone, namely, that there will be a small number of very hard cases which the present concession would not cover, but which could be covered for a matter of a few hundred pounds a year. The fact that these few cases would be in some ways the "hardest" of all would of course lend great force to the argument that they too should be covered.'[68]

McIndoe's reply was to send details of the 16 worst burns cases he had at East Grinstead together with harrowing photographs, and a cost estimate for pay during the treatment period of £3,000 *per annum*.

Gradually the Treasury conceded ground, first to 14 months and then to two and a half years, a limit recommended by the Army and Admiralty Medical Services. Peace slowed the process down but finally, in April 1947, the RAF gained the special concession of no time limit on pay for its convalescing officers but only for plastic surgery on aircrew with attributable injuries.[69]

The acceptance of McIndoe's patients first by East Grinstead and then by the RAF were crucial steps along the road to a fully functioning existence for each man outside the town and outside the service. The world outside the hospital and outside the town had to be faced by each patient, but each did so in the uniform of a service which publicly valued the symbolic and practical contribution he could still make to the war effort. This endorsement and attribution of heroism led many in the world outside the hospital to emulate the example set by the people of East Grinstead by welcoming these highly visible casualties into their midst.

Some of the first contacts between the patients of Ward III and the general public came at the behest of the RAF and MAP, when Battle of Britain veterans such as Roy Lane toured aircraft factories encouraging the workers. In a pattern that was to become the norm, such efforts appear to have been successful but with one or two exceptions. In November 1941 the Air Member for Personnel, Philip Babington, wrote to McIndoe on the subject of the factory visits:

'There is always a call for less badly disfigured people to go round factories and talk to workers about the use of their products, and these talks have been found to have a most excellent effect. I think, however, that it would be a mistake to send on this sort of work anybody who is obviously badly knocked about, as it would be trying on the individual and might have an undesirable effect also on the factory workers, many of whom in these days are women.'[70]

No records exist describing the 'undesirable effects' of such visits but the patients themselves were able to cope with the occasional negative reaction – indeed many Guinea Pigs shared the experience of a kindly member of the public drawing them aside and recommending seeing a good plastic surgeon who could sort them out.

As their numbers increased, so too did public awareness. Visits to the hospitals by celebrities were reported in the national press as well as the local papers. Invitations were no longer just to local events and facilities such as the Windmill, the Rainbow Ballroom and Goodwood Races, but to events of national interest in London. As *The Guinea Pig* remembered:

'Parties were always a feature of the Guinea Pig Club but it was not until the numerical strength of the Guinea Pigs was augmented by the

VIEW OF EAST GRINSTEAD
(AS SEEN FROM FLEET STREET)

Specially drawn for *The Guinea Pig*, and donated by *ILLINGWORTH*

bomber crews that Balls needed to be added to the local Picnics and Parties. In effect, 1942 marked a staging point, for from then on London's West End began to exert an ever-increasing importance in the activities of those patients of the QVH agile enough to make the 30 mile trip.

With transport and petrol available through the cunning of a variety of authorities [one East Grinstead theatre nurse remembers siphoning her father's petrol ration], visits to London became more than weekly occurrences. It is here that specific reference must be made to a few benefactors of that time, showbiz folk, who devoted time and effort to ensuring that seats at West End theatres were available every week to a dozen or so Guinea Pigs under treatment at East Grinstead. Elizabeth Allen, Bebe and Ben Lyon and Vera Lynn spring to mind.'[71]

These seats were often the best in the house and, soon, few theatre premieres were complete without a party of Guinea Pigs, escorted to their seats by specially allocated female companions in full public gaze. One such evening was the opening of the film of the George Gershwin musical, *Lady in the Dark*. The star of the production was Ginger Rogers, who received the Guinea Pigs in her dressing room after the performance to sign autographs and pose for photographs.[72] A party of Guinea Pigs also visited Mae West in her revue *Diamond Lil* and and took back signed photographs to Ward III. One nurse who escorted a group to the West End remembered her car being surrounded by members of the public eager for a glimpse of her increasingly famous charges, and flash bulbs going off as though they were film stars.

From 1941 public exposure of East Grinstead patients also came in the form of the first patient memoirs. Geoffrey Page, Tom Gleave and Bill Simpson all published books between 1941 and 1944 which left the reader in no doubt about the nature of their injuries, the challenges of reconstruction and the extraordinary contribution of all at East Grinstead. Whilst all of these were best sellers, running into several editions, their impact was obscured by Richard Hillary's metaphysical memoir, *The Last Enemy*. Hillary's book was far more ambitious than its fellows, and found an enthusiastic audience amongst the cultural elites. Its reviews were ecstatic, and even McIndoe himself called the book

'... the most outstanding literary contribution of the war in any service ... not only a work of art but, because it gave significance and deep meaning to the lives of thousands of young men, less articulate than himself, who in an age of doubt and near despair could still their inner fears and questionings with nothing but blind courage.'[73]

Hillary's death in a crash in January 1943 provoked paroxysms of grief amongst cultural commentators such as Cyril Connolly who referred to him as 'a phenomenon' and reminded his readers that, at the very least,

'Hillary was fortunate, if there can be any fortune in so short a life, in that he enjoyed literary success before he died.'[74] His most notable memorial was Arthur Koestler's lengthy essay 'The Birth of a Myth' which was voted, by a margin of 2:1, the most popular piece in *Horizon* for the war years by its readership. A more rational assessment of Hillary's work came from the authors of *Since 1939* who noted the generally poor quality of many of the war memoirs:

'This failure is most evident in the reminiscences of airmen who, because their adventures were without precedent and their lives a strange blend of relatively comfortable security on earth and fearful jeopardy in the sky, were more prolific writers than soldiers or sailors. It is not entirely redeemed by the best known of all the books directly inspired by personal experience of air warfare – *The Last Enemy*, by Richard Hillary, one of the few fighter-pilots to whom so many owed so much in the Battle of Britain. This moving testament of youth, grown old beyond its years in single-handed combat with the enemy, is the kind of book which disarms criticism. The obvious defects of its qualities are too firmly woven into the emotional pattern to be isolated, without damaging the texture of the work as a whole. There is, furthermore, the difficulty of estimating how much its appeal owes to the existence, in embryo, of a "Hillary" myth. Like Rupert Brooke in the First World War, Richard Hillary in the second has been chosen as a symbol of youth's tragic destiny and unfulfilled promise.'[75]

The fascination with Richard Hillary has resulted in many biographical studies (see Further Reading) and there is therefore no need to repeat their detail – except, perhaps, to add and to remind that Hillary was an enthusiastic and supportive member of the Guinea Pig Club and not always the lone, troubled crusader as he is often portrayed. Like McIndoe, Hillary could be difficult and self-centred, but at East Grinstead he established close friendships with his fellow patients and so was included in the original group that gathered in the June sun to inaugurate the club. And, for the purposes of this study, Hillary's importance lies in his particular contribution to the multitude of ways McIndoe's patients were visible in British public and national life. They were at the theatre, in the bookshops, at the races, in the factories, in the dancehalls and in the press, both popular and, largely thanks to *The Last Enemy*, highbrow. With this ever-increasing visibility and with East Grinstead as exemplar, merely being in their presence was seen as making a contribution to the war effort, realising McIndoe's prediction in his first *Guinea Pig* magazine contribution 'Message from the Maestro' that:

'... while alone they may have difficulty in holding an honoured position in the community of men, out of their united strength they can find the opportunities and facilities to achieve it.'[76]

A recent interview with a Ward III nurse revealed that Hillary may have been responsible for other, less orthodox contributions to the lives of those associated with the Guinea Pig Club. During her service at East Grinstead, Nurse Rosemary Parkes remembered how one night in 1944:

'I was having my half hour's rest on a theatre trolley in the corridor on Ward III during a spell of night duty when a curious incident occurred. I was woken up by what I took to be Staff Nurse Loftus standing over me in her white uniform and flowing white cap urging me to get up. Glancing at my watch I hurried into the Staff Room to ask "Lofty" why she had woken me up too soon. Her reply was: "I've not been anywhere near you – what you saw must have been the ghost of Richard Hillary."'

It was well known amongst the hospital staff that, in addition to a certain truculence of manner, Hillary had particularly disliked seeing nurses rest and took some pleasure in disturbing their sleep. Apparently even after death Hillary continued his antics and, despite their unsuperstitious practicality, the nurses tolerated him just as they had when he lived.

Geoffrey Page showed this cartoon to Boris Karloff when Page
(Nigel Bruce's son-in-law) was in Hollywood. Karloff loved it

The Guinea Pig Club attracted sustained attention from the other Allied
Forces. Although Geoffrey Page and Richard Hillary had both given radio
interviews in the United States in the early part of the war, their burned
faces were kept out of the American press for fear of alarming the civilian population.

Cover of the very first *Guinea Pig* magazine issued in April 1944.
Note that the cartoon shows fighter pilots chasing down V1s
which had begun to plague the south east of England

By 1944 there was no such fear, and Martha Gellhorn's lengthy article
for *Collier's* magazine was accompanied by a large photograph which
clearly showed injured men in various stages of treatment at East
Grinstead. The hospital's work had made a considerable impression on
Gellhorn, who was considered one of the greatest Allied war correspondents (and at the time was married to Ernest Hemingway). She included
the essay in the anthology of her wartime journalism:

'The hospital is a marvel. The men have unbounded confidence in the surgeons. This confidence is based on observation. They see with their own eyes the slow, patient miracles performed by Doctor Archibald McIndoe. He works with them tirelessly, operating three or five days a week, sometimes from ten in the morning until ten at night. But he does more than surgery, and that is why the hospital is a marvel. You would never see a more delicate and unpretentious job of life-saving than goes on here...

It is natural that these boys should not be thinking much about the peace and how to prevent the Germans from ever starting another war. They have done their share. They have paid for the safety of our world in advance.'[77]

The status and honour accorded the community at East Grinstead was given the ultimate sanction in December 1945 when the King's first post-war Christmas message was immediately preceded by a broadcast live from the Ward III Christmas party. The BBC announcer introduced the broadcast with the words, 'Of all the hospitals in this country, the Queen Victoria is world-famed, and airmen of all nations have found rest, peace and healing there.' The Guinea Pig song was sung and McIndoe made a speech in which, 'We of Ward III wish you all a Merry Christmas', ending with the plea that the public should, 'not forget these boys who come to us here at East Grinstead from all over the world.'[78]

Chapter Seven

The Privilege of Living

'Real and lasting satisfaction... is derived from... what the patient does with what the surgeon achieves, rather than from the purely technical aspect of the repair.'[1]

After the war, any concerns that Archibald McIndoe may have had about his charges at East Grinstead being forgotten were unfounded. Yet whilst the public memory proved itself to be durable, it also proved itself to be compliant in a complex process whereby an official version of the war – particularly the air war – replaced much of recent historical reality. Despite the fact that it was the great engines of bombers that thundered over their homes nearly every night for nearly four years, in the public memory this most modern of offensive campaigns all but disappeared almost immediately the conflict was over. Instead the work of the Royal Air Force was reordered to conform to a Great War model of fighters and aces and dog-fights and defence, ensuring that it was the Battle of Britain that came to stand for the entire air war. As a recent historian of Bomber Command put it, 'The government started a campaign of forgetting... the British State found it politic to blame Harris and eventually took the British people with it.'[2] Unsurprisingly the Guinea Pig Club has always been numbered among the staunchest defenders of Arthur Harris, and marked the installation of his statue outside the RAF church of St Clement Danes with an editorial entitled 'A Wrong Put Right'.[3]

This process of reordering the history of the air war had very particular consequences for the position of the Guinea Pig Club in the post-war period. The great heroism demonstrated by the 647 Guinea Pigs in both the experience of injury and of reconstruction had been a matter of tremendous and persistent public acclaim throughout the war years. Such heroism could not be circumscribed or qualified so that it only applied to the 20 per cent of the club from Fighter Command. Instead the process of sacrifice, by which faces were lost in the flames, became conflated with the process of sacrifice that underscored the mythology of the Battle of Britain. In effect the Guinea Pigs all became fighter aces, returning to a more classical model of individual heroism in combat, that easily resonated with their heroism in injury – the many became 'The Few.'[4] Typically, a 1948 article in *Time* magazine could write, in a profile of McIndoe, 'As the Battle of Britain raged, some 4,500 airmen were pulled out of their wrecked and flaming planes.'[5]

That this process happened so quickly and completely was partly due to pre-existing conditions in the Guinea Pig Club itself. Fighter pilot Richard Hillary's *The Last Enemy* had become the literary symbol of the Guinea Pig Club, despite the existence of several other works by club members which, whilst not having the longevity of Hillary's work, sold equally well during the war years. As we have seen, Archibald McIndoe himself called the book, 'the most outstanding literary contribution of the war in any service', although his piece for the *National and English Review* made no mention of Hillary's service specifics.[6] Thus post-war analysts of the bombing campaign were able to claim that:

'... the [strategic bombing] campaign lacks a chronicle to rank with *Winged Victory*, *The Last Enemy*, or *Flight to Arras*... It has no Richard Hillary, certainly no Day Lewis or St Exupery.'[7]

There is, however, no evidence that Hillary intended his work to be specifically about Fighter Command, and it should be remembered that at the time of his death Hillary was retraining to fly night bombers.

The first article attacking the manipulation of public memory in this way was published in *The Guinea Pig* in August 1948. Editor Henry Standen, injured when his mine-laying Hampden caught fire on the runway, wrote:

'The so-called "popular press" has a penchant for writing up sentimental and often quite unrecognisable stories about Guinea Pigs...

Having been very badly bitten by a journalist to whom I gave a perfectly honest interview, I feel strongly about this matter. I gave this Fleet Street type the truth, the whole truth and nothing but the truth; but the story that was published (complete with photograph) shook me and mine stark rigid. In course of transcribing the notes, the newshound had turned me from an ordinary member of a Bomber Squadron into a top line Battle of Britain fighter ace. I don't have to dwell on the embarrassment it caused... Golly, if I could have got hold of that wretched journalist, no plastic surgeon would have been able to put him right again...'[8]

Twenty years later the producers of the 1969 film *The Battle of Britain* used Guinea Pig Bill Foxley to play a burned squadron leader from Fighter Command working in an operations room.[9] As part of the plot he is introduced to a fellow squadron leader's wife, played by Susanna York. York later remembered the occasion for a recent history of the Battle of Britain:

'I hadn't realised that his hands had been so badly burned. I only heard afterwards about how Battle of Britain pilots used to take their gloves off to get better control of their planes, and then – when the fire started – they... Anyway, I took his hand and I realised what the whole ordeal must have been like.'[10]

What neither the film-makers, his fellow actors, or the editors of the anthology appear to have realised is that Foxley was a navigator on a Wellington bomber which crashed during training, burning his face and hands away when he went back to help his crewmates (he had escaped from the aircraft relatively unscathed). Foxley came from a working class Liverpool background, with a Scouse accent that he retains today. During the making of *The Battle of Britain* he had to adopt the cut-glass tones of a typical officer of Fighter Command, but in post-production it was felt that his accent lacked the right tone and he was summoned to an editing studio to dub his own voice to the director's satisfaction. This year, as ever, Bill Foxley will lead the Guinea Pig contingent on the march past the Cenotaph on Remembrance Sunday.

Complications of a different kind were in store for the foreign Guinea Pigs who had been injured and reconstructed in Britain, away from their homelands. This was especially true for the largest group (125) from Canada who were returning for the first time to a nation which had no real idea of what to expect. The process of accommodation would have to begin all over again in a population whose experience of war, and of its casualties, had been remote.

The Canadian response to the issue of its returning burn casualties was as unique as it was imaginative. Joining forces with the National Film Board of Canada, in 1944 an RCAF production team arrived at East Grinstead to film the story of *New Faces Come Back*, a fictionalised account of the life of 'Jim' a Canadian fitter turned flight engineer, whose burn injuries take him to East Grinstead where he is reconstructed prior to repatriation to Canada. The film that resulted deserves to be better known as it is quite simply one of a kind in cinematographic history. Lasting half an hour, it was designed as a public information message, to be shown in cinemas after the newsreel and before the main feature. The writer of the film, Cecil Maiden, was British but the producer and director were all Canadian and together they produced a remarkably engaging and effective piece of work. Canadian audiences were gradually and carefully made aware of the sort and sight of disfigurement suffered by some of their servicemen who would soon be back home amongst them, and exhorted to match the efforts of the British. The film began with an introduction from Edward Blacksell, the real life welfare officer at East Grinstead but over-dubbed with a Canadian accent. He began by telling his audience:

'I am a welfare officer at a hospital that is still refitting for the peace the men wrecked by war... they are returning to you to try to make a comeback in your world.'

Emphasis was placed on the example of East Grinstead's relationship with its patients (and subtle comparisons with egalitarian Canada were drawn):

'At first the quiet English countryside didn't understand our work at the hospital... the war had not yet torn down the jealous privacies of England... '

Then the town's acceptance and assistance was shown in a variety of vignettes of the kindly yet eccentric townsfolk. Jim got over his operation thanks to their help and attended town social events where, 'for the first time he was called upon to use, in front of strangers, his burned and broken hands'. The character of Jim was played by English wireless operator/navigator Jack Allaway and, although his face was shown bandaged for most of the film, his hands (with the badly damaged fingers) were displayed prominently. All goes well for Jim until the factory dance (outside East Grinstead) where he is brutally rejected by a female co-worker ('who wants to be held by that sort of thing?'). Jim returns to the hospital where his self-confidence is restored to him and for the first time the audience is shown in great detail the full extent of the consequences of burn injuries on his fellow patients. The camera lingers on face after face, showing scarring, blinding, post-operative disfigurement, tube pedicles connecting face to shoulder, and missing eyes and hands.

His confidence restored by contact with the patient community, Jim prepares to return home to Canada. At this point the challenge is made to the Canadian population, presumably by now determined to outdo the English example. As Jim's girlfriend kisses him on the mouth as his train steams away, the welfare officer tells the audience:

'In his stay with us Jim had found good neighbours and friends. Now homeward bound he wondered whether it would be easy to pick up old friendships... but they found that the man behind the mask was the same man with the laughter undamaged, the hope undimmed... Canada bound, one of a crowd. His new life lies ahead. If he finds the same friendship and understanding as he did with us, his comeback will be quick. We in our hospital have done our best for him. The rest is up to you.'

Aided by Canadian government regulations which guaranteed employment and education rights for veterans, McIndoe and Tilley's Canadian army did indeed make quick comebacks. Many joined the civilian air services: Paul Warren became an air traffic controller at Manitoba airport, and Frank Hanton DFC became general manager of aviation for the Government of Saskatchewan, after his initial posting in the department responsible for fighting fires from the air. Larry Somers trained as a vet, and both Bill Martin and Leo Tremblay joined the Department of Veterans Affairs. An amputee himself, Leo worked in the Prosthetic Services department in Quebec City where, despite his regret at never having seen active service, he felt he was finally able to make his own valuable contribution to the war effort. Ross Tilley, by 1945 a wing commander and holder of an OBE, returned to take up a position in plastic surgery at Toronto's Wellesley Hospital. In 1982 he was given the Order of Canada. Today the hospital is as proud as ever of its connection with Tilley and his most celebrated group of patients, naming its burns unit after him. One of the largest in Canada, it has 14 intensive care beds, its own operating theatre and facilities and is used to train trauma care professionals from all over the country. Tilley died in 1988.

The courage and determination of the men of the RCAF continues to draw the interest of their fellow countrymen. In 2001 a television documentary, entitled *The Guinea Pig Club: The Reconstruction of Burned Airmen in World War Two*, told the story of the Canadian branch of the Guinea Pig Club. The programme gained high ratings and four awards, including one for best historical documentary of 2002.[11]

In Britain, despite the complexities of their misrepresentation, 'McIndoe's Army' were indeed remembered and valued as they sought to negotiate their position in peacetime society. Although the 'excitement and stimulus' of wartime had gone, the enthusiasm for the work of the hospital was unabated, and McIndoe's work continued to receive and generate publicity, both international and national. In August 1946 Winston Churchill himself invited a select group of Guinea Pigs (three out of four of whom were bomber crewmen) to his residence near Geneva during a club trip to Switzerland. Hugh Dowding, Arthur Harris and especially Charles Portal maintained what was to be their lifelong support for the club. Guinea Pig Paul Hart appeared on *Have a Go*, a hugely popular radio quiz show, hosted by Wilfred Pickles, which toured the country interviewing local celebrities. When Hart stepped up to the microphone Pickles said, 'I usually ask people if they have been in the services, but it is pretty obvious you were.' Pickles praised Hart's courage and his enterprise in starting up a successful bulb business, earning himself a reprimand from the BBC for advertising. When the programme celebrated its 150th edition, Hart and fellow Guinea Pig, Dicky Richardson, appeared again.[12]

Abroad, the reputation of East Grinstead was proving to be equally durable. In 1948 *Time* magazine marked a lecture tour by McIndoe with an article on 'The Man Who Makes Faces'.[13] Ten years later McIndoe made the news in Hollywood when Ava Gardner fell from a horse injuring her face. The star of *Pandora and the Flying Dutchman*, *The Barefoot Contessa*, *Showboat*, *Mogambo* and *Bhowani Junction* developed a haematoma on her cheekbone that failed to subside. Gardner devoted six pages to the episode in her autobiography so her contact with McIndoe and his patients clearly had a profound effect on her. After her injury Gardner realised:

'I needed Archie McIndoe. So I went to see [him] at his East Grinstead hospital for the Royal Air Force... I knew that in comparison to what was going on with those badly burned pilots, my little injury was of almost no consequence. But Archie was a man of enormous compassion and understanding, and he had enough to spare for me... I sat there and looked at the man who was probably the greatest plastic surgeon in the world, let out a breath and waited for his advice.'

McIndoe assured the owner of one of the most beautiful faces in the world that the haematoma would eventually go down of its own accord and that intervention could possibly make it worse. Ignoring the advice of another surgeon sent to her by the studios, Gardner let nature take its course and:

'As Archie prophesied, the lump slowly subsided, though I was always conscious that it existed and I began to fear that my film career might be over. I continued to visit Archie and I became more involved with those badly mutilated pilots. It was the best possible therapy for me, because compared with their injuries, my lump couldn't have been more insignificant. What Archie did for those boys my words can never adequately describe... I met a lot of them and we danced and laughed together. They were so brave I could have wept. Archie told me my visits did them a lot of good, but I'm sure they helped me more than I ever helped them.'[14]

The feeling was mutual. When Gardner opened a hospital fete for McIndoe after her recovery the Guinea Pigs told her they had voted her, 'the girl they most wanted to get a graft from'. And when Gardner told them she had actually eaten guinea pigs in Spain, one club member concluded that this would be 'a beautiful way to die'.[15]

The history of the British Guinea Pigs from the end of the war right up until the present day, despite the obscuring of the bombers' war, is extraordinarily rich and varied. It even includes several new club members who joined after 1945. Harry Williams was injured in occupied Hamburg in 1946 when his vehicle was deliberately rammed by a lorry, throwing him into a tree and leaving him with a fractured skull and severe facial injuries. Transferred almost immediately to East Grinstead, he spent almost a year being reconstructed and then joined the Ministry of Works until his retirement in 1977. Keith Base got through the war intact but in 1947, still in the RAF, he was carrying out rocket firing tests when the engine of his Spitfire packed up. Keith crashed and during the belly landing, smashed his face against his gun sight. Keith was one of the last patients at the RAF unit at Rauceby before transferring to East Grinstead. His reconstruction was not completed until 1950, when he was invalided out of the RAF (although not before he had married an East Grinstead nurse). He completed a degree at Harper Adams agricultural college and then joined the Massey Ferguson company as a lecturer in its educational department.

Probably the most remarkable story of a Guinea Pig in the post-war period is that of Joe Capka, a member of 311 (Czech) Squadron. Unlike all his fellow Pigs, the scars on Joe's face that bore witness to his military service had the most appalling consequences for both him and his family.

Joe Capka

Joe arrived in Britain via Poland and the French Air Service in 1940. By 1942 he was flying night fighters and getting to know Rhoda, a young radio operator who often guided him home. They were married on D-Day. Joe joined the Guinea Pig Club three weeks after he was married when his Mosquito was fired upon by a German plane. Almost blinded, he persuaded his observer to bale out and then crash landed the aircraft on English soil, badly burned and 'mashed' (in Guinea Pig parlance) in the ensuing explosion. Months of treatment at East Grinstead followed which restored the sight in his right eye and reconstructed his face and body. Up to this point, Joe's story was typical but on his return to Czechoslovakia after the war, things became a great deal darker. For the first couple of years Joe and Rhoda established a normal life, with Joe serving as a captain in the Czech Air Force.

In 1948 the ruling Communist regime expelled from military service anyone who had fought in the Western Allies' forces. In the same week Joe sought and was refused permission to leave the country, as well as being awarded the Croix de Guerre for his work in the French Air Service – recognition that made his situation even worse. Instead he decided to escape, but the attempt went wrong and Joe and other former servicemen were charged with treason and sentenced to ten years' hard labour, the first to be spent in solitary confinement. Rhoda was deported and returned to Britain. Years in the brutal prison camp system followed, details of which can be seen in a recent Czech film, *Dark Blue World*, which told of the horrifying travesties of justice that were visited on heroes like Joe by their own countrymen. After two failed appeals, Joe finally made it out of Czechoslovakia in May 1957 and rejoined Rhoda in England. His book, *Red Sky at Night*, was the first to tell of what had happened to him and his fellow Czechs when they returned, and he drew further attention to their plight when he appeared on *This is Your Life* in 1958. The remainder of his life was spent quietly with his family in Essex, and a lifelong employment as an electrical engineer.

Few other Guinea Pigs had quite such extraordinary or harrowing post-war lives as Joe Capka, except perhaps for fighter pilot Jackie Mann. Based with 91 Squadron at Hawkinge during the Battle of Britain, Mann was shot down five times in 1940 and 1941. On his sixth time, Mann was forced to glide home from over the Channel. His aircraft crashed and burst into flames, burning him severely into the bargain. Mann managed to exit his craft, take pictures of it, and then walk off towards the nearest farmhouse for help. He was a founding member of the Guinea Pig Club and on its original committee. After the war, so that he might keep on flying, Mann and his wife Sunnie left for Cyprus where he took up charter piloting. As the years went by, the pages of *The Guinea Pig* recorded his move to the Middle East and his career in civil aviation there. On his retirement from flying Mann and Sunnie decided to stay in their adopted country and he continued to keep his fellow club members up to date with his life. After his entry in the magazine for January 1983 *The Guinea Pig* noted with some concern that he was, 'still living in that hotspot, Lebanon'. Soon after Mann became one of the British hostages, along with Terry Waite and John McCarthy. After 865 days in captivity, Mann was finally released, and his homecoming lit up the Club's 50th anniversary celebrations. Sadly, almost three years of captivity, including starvation and regular beatings, meant that this redoubtable veteran, with his handlebar moustache worn as proudly as the scars on his face, lived to enjoy only a few extra years of freedom.

No Guinea Pig would say that his re-entry into society was problem free, and almost all had to endure some difficulties in their encounters with members of the public not as well informed as those of East Grinstead. (Several reported being asked if they were worried if they would pass on their conditions to their children!) For some the severity of their injuries, whether directly related to their burning or indirectly, meant that they were unable to return to the full professional life they had either had, or anticipated, before the war. Bill Warman's internal injuries caused by the ingestion of large amounts of petrol blighted his life and Les Syrett's orthopaedic injuries caused him lifelong problems. For those Guinea Pigs who needed extra support, their club liaised with the RAF Benevolent Fund to ensure that they got it, thereby fulfilling one of the original pledges made in June 1941 to, 'focus the attention of responsible bodies on the needs of injured aircrew'.[16] Similarly the Club has an Honorary Plastic Surgeon attached to it to assist with any health problems its members may have (in Britain Tom Cochrane and in Canada Leith Douglas) and to attend to any follow-up action necessitated by the problems of ageing grafted skin. For some surgeons trained at East Grinstead, post-war responsibilities could be more gruelling than during the conflict. RAFMS Maxillo-Facial surgeon Nigel Dutt, now married to his theatre nurse Dorothy, was often required to identify aircrew recovered from crashed aircraft by the remains of their jaw bones or dental plates. This painstaking, difficult work went on for years as wreckage was found into the 1950s. Dutt's family remembered how distressing it could be, especially on one occasion when his results were lost by the RAF and he was obliged to start all over again.

Notwithstanding the occasional setbacks, the vast majority of the

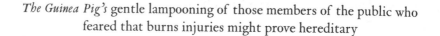

"Are they all yours, old man?"

The Guinea Pig's gentle lampooning of those members of the public who
feared that burns injuries might prove hereditary

Guinea Pigs were able to return to civilian and public life with very little
difficulty, many resuming or starting full family and professional lives.
Derek Martin, the 'web-footed Guinea Pig', was given command of a jet
fighter station in 1951 but persistent problems from his wartime injuries
ended his front line flying career (he paid several visits to East Grinstead
during the 1950s to have his left tear duct widened as it regularly became
obstructed by scar tissue causing constant watering and obstructed

vision). He became a signals specialist, ending a distinguished RAF career at NATO HQ. His love for Sunderlands never diminished and later, during his still hectic retirement, he arranged for a Sunderland to make one of only two landings ever on the Thames.

A substantial number of British and Canadian Guinea Pigs went to work for civilian airlines – it appears that this industry, like the RAF, 'did not want to waste this class of personnel'. Among them, Ken Brown was one of the first civilian air traffic controllers at Heathrow, and Bill Simpson and Geoffrey Page both went to work for aircraft manufacturers.

Peter Weekes became a headmaster (at a prep school attended by the children of Richard Dimbleby). Vic Hobbs sold fire extinguishers – *The Guinea Pig* magazine bemoaned when it reported his appointment, 'Why oh why didn't we meet that man before?'[17] Ian Craig returned to his pre-war job as a fire insurance surveyor. Alan Morgan returned to engineering (although the process was problematic – during his successful interview he kept both hands in his pockets and it was only several weeks into his appointment that his company noticed he had lost eight fingers to frostbite). Bertram Owen-Smith had been an insurance clerk before the war; after it he trained and practised as a plastic surgeon. A blinded Jimmy Wright ceased his career as a cameraman and instead started a production company based at Twickenham Studios. Edward Scott (like Wright one of the 16 worst cases) returned to his job at the Prudential Insurance company, and Noel Newman resumed his medical career. Jack Perry trained as a draftsman, joining first Plessey and then the Atomic Energy Research Establishment at Harwell.

The breadth of public acceptance and acknowledgement of what each Guinea Pig stood for remained a remarkable feature of the post-war landscape and beyond. Even companies in the service sector were prepared to put the needs of their disfigured employees above the sensibilities of their customers. Marks and Spencer was a case in point. Jack Toper (the longest-serving editor of *The Guinea Pig*) joined the company in 1946 and was sent to the Economic Research Department at the Baker Street head office. After his six weeks of initial training he decided he preferred the atmosphere of the sales floor and approached personnel to effect a transfer. Without any objection at all Toper became a 'store man' rising through the ranks and becoming a store manager.[18] Although customer reaction could be difficult, the company gave total support to Toper and several other Guinea Pigs it employed. This reflected the close relationship between

Archibald McIndoe and Sir Simon Marks, who had been an early supporter of East Grinstead through his sister Elaine, Mrs Neville Blond, who opened her Sussex home to the patients of Ward III and provided some of the earliest and most sustained financial support. As well as donating the Tannoy system and curtains for the.hospital wards, the family also enabled McIndoe's research foundation, the Blond-McIndoe, to come into existence. M&S advertised in every issue of *The Guinea Pig*.

The behaviour of Britain's most successful retail company was by no means exceptional. In April 1960, on the last night of his life, McIndoe sat next to Billy Butlin at a dinner at the Dorchester. He asked if there were jobs for Guinea Pigs available in Butlin's holiday camp organisation and Butlin replied that there were. The next day Jack Allaway and Tommy Brandon were contacted by Butlin's executive Bernard Jenkins about an interview. Allaway had been on his way to Cunard as a junior purser but the Butlin's posting to its Clacton camp suited his family much better (Brandon went to Phwelli). Allaway took up an administrative post (despite his starring role in *New Faces Come Back* he felt he lacked the requisite show business skills to be a Redcoat) and performed well enough for Butlin to offer him a job in the flagship Butlin's development in the Bahamas. Allaway turned it down as he did not wish to disrupt his family life – a sensible choice as the Bahamas project ultimately failed.[19]

There were many other places where the Guinea Pigs and reminders of their achievements could be found. In 1952 the Imperial War Museum took out a subscription to *The Guinea Pig* and now holds a complete set of the magazine from its inception in 1944. In July 1990 a Mk 5 Spitfire (AB910) of the Battle of Britain Memorial Flight was dedicated to the Guinea Pig Club and flies today with the club brevet painted on its fuselage. Four Guinea Pigs have also appeared on *This Is Your Life* between 1961 and 1988 (Bill Simpson, Geoffrey Page, Tom Gleave and Joe Capka). One of the more unusual examples of continuing public awareness came in 1982 when the club was approached by some film-makers from Channel 4 and asked if it could provide some ravaged looking extras to play down-and-outs for a drama. Jack Toper immediately volunteered and spent three days at Stonebridge Park Railway staggering about looking suitably wrecked and meeting the requirements of the producers perfectly.[20]

Because of its continuing association with East Grinstead (the club's annual meetings are held in the town and many members live in the south-east), Guinea Pigs are often to be found at the hospital encouraging the victims of burns found in its wards today. Nor have the members of the club forgotten the military context of their injuries. Remarkably, there have been Guinea Pigs associated with the casualties of every major war fought by British servicemen since 1945. In 1982 the Club volunteered its services to help the casualties of the Falklands conflict, among whom were 47 severely burned men, most of whom were Welsh Guardsmen who had been trapped on HMS *Sir Galahad*. *The Guinea Pig* recorded a visit by several club members to the Falklands burn cases at both Woolwich and Haslar military infirmaries. The Pigs were:

'... welcomed and of course were able to pass on some useful tips, such as, the necessity for continuous finger exercises, thus preventing joints from stiffening. Some of them showed concern, in case burned fingers could leave them with premature arthritis. We quickly dispelled those fears. We even donned sterile gowns and overshoes to visit the saline baths... '[21]

Chief Guinea Pig Tom Gleave formed a close relationship with the very worst (and most famous) burns case of the Falklands conflict, Simon Weston. Gleave and the other club members were able to provide a great deal of support and encouragement to Weston, who repaid him with a heartfelt tribute when Gleave was the subject of *This Is Your Life*, calling him his greatest hero. Flight Lieutenant John Nichol, held as a PoW in the first Gulf War, acknowledged the continuing debt of all servicemen to the hospital by becoming Chairman of the Friends of the Blond-McIndoe research trust. And Sam Gallop, whose injuries included double leg amputation as well as serious burns, not only founded the charity Employment Opportunities with its very 'McIndoe-ist' aim of meaningful professional lives for disabled people, but is also a senior figure in the Limbless Association. Gallop chairs the association's 'Empower' committee, and was partly responsible for bringing Ali Abbas to Britain from

Iraq to have prosthetic limbs fitted following his injuries in the bombing during the second Gulf War.[22]

And finally, after 60 years, the landscape of public memory that the Guinea Pigs inhabit has started to resemble the reality of the air war of 1939–45, and not some officially preferable mythologised version. The research and writing of this book has coincided with a long overdue public acknowledgement of the contribution of Bomber Command to the Second World War. Marginalised for over half of the 20th century, its men and the work they did are finally receiving the attention they deserve in the 21st. This attention is not coming just from a new generation of historians, but also from a new *visibility* in the public sphere. Suddenly its men and machines are everywhere: in 2002 the last flying Lancaster bomber flew with two Spitfires during the state funeral for HM The Queen Mother. This was the first time a Lancaster had been seen flying over London for 50 years, and public reaction to it was as warm as it was to its fighter escorts (it flew again during the Jubilee celebrations in 2003). And in April 2002, 60 years after the first 'thousand bomber raids', the first Service of Remembrance specifically for the dead of Bomber Command was held at Westminster Abbey.

Conclusions

'I usually ask people if they have been in the Services, but it is pretty obvious you were.'

Wilfred Pickles to Guinea Pig Paul Hart, BBC Radio, 1948

This book came about for a number of reasons; primarily it has sought to understand a unique phenomenon in the British experience of the Second World War, when men with severe facial disfigurements became an accepted, even celebrated feature of the wartime landscape.

It is not an exaggeration to state that the Guinea Pig Club was unique. It had no equivalent in either the British Army or the Royal Navy, or in any of the other Allied armed forces, before or since. Before 1940 it had been standard behaviour by the armed forces to contain their most disfigured casualties away from public gaze. Had the RAF wished to suppress or minimise the public exposure of its burned servicemen it could have done so (albeit with some effort and a great deal of hospital relocation), and no amount of pressure from Archibald McIndoe or anyone else could have made any difference. RAFGH Matlock, which provided the psychiatric facilities for disturbed aircrew, was located miles away from anywhere or anyone on the Derbyshire Moors, and what went on there remains, 'a deeply obscured subject'.[1]

Part of the process of understanding the story of Archibald McIndoe and the Guinea Pig Club has been to connect it, for the first time, to wider histories of Britain in the Second World War, and in particular to histories of the Royal Air Force. It is important to remember this very specific service context as often histories concerned with the Home Front see little beyond the influence of the Beveridge Report of 1942. And whilst ideas about fundamental social reform post-war were among the leading topics of conversation in the period, the debates about the future of burned RAF aircrew were not part of this 'wartime reformist consensus'.[2]

The RAF's engagement with the consequences of burn injuries to its servicemen took place entirely within a military framework. There was no reference whatsoever to the civilian state assuming responsibility for these men, indeed it was seen as preferable that the RAF should look after its own, even after the war was ended. The moral responsibility and duty that was emphasised at the highest levels of the service came not from religious or social convictions, but from convictions about how wars should be fought. This is a history in which the burned airmen of the RAF are symbols, not of the new peace, but of the new war.

Each member of the Guinea Pig Club was the visual confirmation of the heavy responsibilities he and his service had borne on behalf of their countrymen as part of those convictions about a new kind of war. The extent of their injuries symbolised the extent to which they had defended millions of ordinary citizens from the enemy and spared them from the rigours of land-based conflict. The RAF believed that it had found the very best of men to shoulder such a burden and the quality of this new model army of technical specialists demanded the very best of care in return. Therefore the coincidence of Archibald McIndoe with the RAF's commitment to its aircrew was truly remarkable. At East Grinstead he created a therapeutic environment that successfully reconstructed not only the heroes of the new war, but the very concept of heroism itself, and in doing so successfully reinterpreted the RAF concepts of war and responsibility.

The public response to McIndoe's patients was a confirmation to the RAF that its conception and operation of this new kind of war were recognised and accepted as significantly altering the nature of public participation in combat. By acknowledging even the war's most disfigured casualties, people also acknowledged the necessity of their responsibility and their sacrifice. As the RAF had hoped, the new relationships between the RAF and its servicemen in turn generated a new relationship between the public and the service as a whole. So, as well as Beveridge's more celebrated version, it appears there was a second, militarily specific, social contract in Britain in the 1940s. This was the contract between defender and the defended, and one of its most important terms was the security of care and of recognition for those who had sacrificed the most to spare the majority.

A secondary aim of this book has been to contribute a new perspective to the histories of the British Home Front in the Second World War – histories which in the case of the relationships between the Home Front and the Royal Air Force are often skewed and incomplete. The 'campaign of forgetting' about the strategic air offensive is a significant reason why the relationship between the RAF and the British public is frequently misrepresented. In the main Bomber Command has been isolated from general histories of the war, which instead focus on the activities of one small part of the service, Fighter Command. In the words of one British aviation historian, 'the many became the Few', (and this tendency can be seen in microcosm with the treatment in public memory of the members of the Guinea Pig Club).[3] This is not only unfair, it is inaccurate and unrepresentative of reality between 1939 and 1945. There is no evidence that the RAF, the Air Ministry or the Air Council thought in terms which segregated one command from another. The effort from the Air Force was an integrated whole, with the commands contributing vital, interlinked components to the conception and prosecution of the war. And it should be remembered that for almost four years, apart from the fluctuating fortunes of the armies in North Africa, this was 'the only way of intervening' in a war whose front line was 22 miles from the British coast.[4] In the very recent past, there have been new histories of the bombers' war, but although they provide a long overdue assessment of the men and events of the strategic air offensive, even some of these have a tendency to analyse the activities of the command in isolation from the rest of the war.[5]

There is another significant reason for the misrepresentation of the Home Front which arises from the preoccupation of a number of historians with the events of 1940.[6] The events of the final six months of 1940,

Dunkirk, the Battle of Britain and the Blitz, have come to stand for the entire experience of war for the people of the Home Front. Whether the historians concerned support this interpretation or criticise it, they have made no suggestion for a significant alternative framework for analysing the relationships of the Home Front and the people's war. Furthermore, such analysis perpetuates the marginalisation of Bomber Command from general histories. Thus 'the People's War' is one where the British people are always victims and underdogs, cheerfully but powerlessly going about their business in the face of almost certain defeat until the arrival of the Americans in 1944.

But, the truth of the Second World War should be characterised entirely differently. Far from being ineffective or vulnerable Great Britain was 'a technological and militant nation'.[7] By 1939 Britain was in possession of a strategic weapon of the utmost modernity in concept and operation, in the form of the RAF. This weapon enabled the country to take the war to the enemy for almost five years, despite the fact that the majority of the land army remained in its camps until the middle of 1944.[8] One way that the people of the Home Front were linked to this war was by the highly visible presence in their midst of the patients of Archibald McIndoe. Their acceptance of such injured men marked not only their acceptance of the RAF's mission, but was also their contribution to a war being fought on their behalf. 'The People's War' was not a war in which they were primarily victims, but participants; and if anything, it was the Bombers' War that truly was the People's War.

At the time of writing there were only 120 members of the Guinea Pig Club left out of the original 649. In 2001, the sixtieth anniversary of the founding of the club, the remaining members voted to continue holding their annual meeting at East Grinstead until there are only 50 members remaining, and the last issue of *The Guinea Pig* appeared in the autumn of 2003. Above all, this book was written for them, and for all the men and women associated with the burns units at East Grinstead, Ely, Halton, Cosford and Rauceby, among them my grandmother, VAD Nurse Beryl

Daintry who cared for the boys of Ward III. Their story deserves to be more than just a curiosity of the period; it should be recognised for the value of its contribution to our understanding of the history of Britain at war in the 20th century. This work was inspired by the words of Archibald McIndoe who died, exhausted, in 1960, and is the only civilian to be interred in the RAF church at St Clement Danes:

> 'One day someone will tell the complete story of Ward III in the way it should be told... This future writer will tell of the return of the men from Dunkirk, tired but undismayed who found their first rest there; of the Battle of Britain fought overhead and the burned pilots who came to regard the place as home, gave it its particular flavour and went back to fight carrying a card inscribed "In case of further trouble deliver the bits to Ward III, East Grinstead." He will tell of the Blitz, and of the men, women and children of London and what they thought of it all; of the Bombers' war and the Flying Bomb reply; of D-Day and the return to France... He will tell of the Guinea Pig Club, how and why it started, what it achieved and what has become of all the Guinea Pigs who did not go down to defeat, but rose, from defeat to victory. Perhaps, too, of the vast gifts which came from America, Canada, Australia, South Africa and New Zealand to recognise the sacrifice of those who went back to fight and who encountered The Last Enemy...
>
> This is the story to be told before the name that was Ward III sinks into oblivion. It is a great tale, and worthy of the telling.'
>
> Sir Archibald McIndoe, CBE, MS, MSc, FRCS, FACS.

From 'The Maestro's Message', in The Guinea Pig magazine, April 1948, on the occasion of the closure of Ward III.

Further Reading

This is is by no means a definitive history of the Guinea Pig Club or of the hospital at East Grinstead so, for those wishing to read more details of the people and places appearing in the story, the following will prove useful. Two biographies of Archibald McIndoe have been produced: *McIndoe Plastic Surgeon* by Hugh McLeave and Leonard Mosley's *Faces from the Fire*. Both cover McIndoe's entire life but tend to draw on the same range of rather limited primary material so reading one or the other rather than both is sufficient.

The best body of writing on the subject comes from the Guinea Pigs themselves. Richard Hillary's *The Last Enemy* is of course the most famous but more detail as to the physical reality of life and treatment at East Grinstead may be found in Bill Simpson's *One of Our Pilots is Safe* and *The Way of Recovery*. Geoffrey Page's memoir, *Tale of a Guinea Pig*, was recently reissued as *Shot Down in Flames*. Tom Gleave's contribution, *I had a Row with a German*, is full of interesting detail, and Richard Pape's *Boldness Be My Friend*, with its introduction by Archibald McIndoe, tells of Pape's numerous, usually hopeless, escape attempts from PoW camps as well as his time in Ward III. Colin Hodgkinson's *Best Foot Forward* and John Harding's *Dancing Navigator* give a bomber crewman's perspective, and Robert Wright, biographer of both Hugh Dowding and Sholto Douglas, also wrote of his own time in Ward III in *Night Fighter*. *Red Sky at Night*, Joe Capka's memoir of his ordeal not only by fire but by totalitarian state, is an extraordinary testament to a lifetime of courage. Perhaps the most unusual literary contribution is from Charles MacLean who chose to represent his experiences in novel form. *The Heavens are not too High* is an exciting and gritty story set in besieged Malta, with vivid retellings of the desperate defensive dog-fights and a moving description of one pilot's burning.

Other writing about, rather than by, Guinea Pigs includes Williams and Harrison's *McIndoe's Army: The Injured Airmen who Faced the World*. Edward Bishop was responsible for many of the Guinea Pig obituaries for the *Daily Telegraph* and his work *The Guinea Pig Club* has recently been reissued as *McIndoe's Army*. An anthology, *Five Brave Guinea Pigs* – often misplaced by libraries into their 'Pet Section' – concentrates on the Czech patients of Ward III. David Ross' biography of Richard Hillary recycles much of the material mentioned above for its section on his injuries so Sebastian Faulks' section on Hillary in his collective biography *The Fatal Englishman* is probably a shorter and more original read. Anthony Dennison's *A Cottage Hospital Grows Up: The Story of the Queen Victoria Hospital* details the history of the hospital at East Grinstead itself from its inception until the 1960s. Two of the plastic surgeons who passed through McIndoe's unorthodox training programme both during and after the war have written about their experiences: Jack Penn in *The Right to Look Human* and Benjamin Rank in *Heads and Hands: An Era of Plastic Surgery*.

Histories of Allied PoWs in Germany that are not preoccupied with escapes are remarkably thin on the ground. Bob Moore and Kent Fedorowich are among a very few who give the subject serious academic consideration in *Prisoners of War and their Captors in World War II*, as is David Rolf in his work *Prisoners of the Reich: Germany's Captives, 1939–1945*. Several PoW doctors have written of their experiences however, and their memoirs give a good picture of the details of ordinary PoW existence. Leslie Le Souef's *To War without a Gun* is one such work, and John Borrie's *Despite Captivity: a Doctor's Life at War* and Ion Ferguson's *Doctor at War* are good examples, and both mention the work of David Charters. Lord Hussey's biography, *Chance Governs All*, gives the longest description of life at Bad Soden, and complete sets of *The Prisoner of War* magazine are available as two bound volumes in the reading room of the Imperial War Museum. German medical expertise fell increasingly short of that of the Allies, particularly in the fields of treatment for shock and blood transfusions. The reasons for this are made clear in Mark Kater's excellent *Doctors Under Hitler* and Pross and Aly's *The Value of the Human Being:*

Medicine in Germany, 1918 to 1945. The most recent history of Allied PoWs in Germany, *The Last Escape,* comes from John Nichol and Tony Rennell and their bibliography contains many useful pointers for those wishing to follow up on what is still a very under-researched period.

For a general history of the Royal Air Force, John Terraine's *The Right of the Line* is unlikely ever to be surpassed. However, I have also drawn on some of the newer historiographical thinking in my conception of the Royal Air Force as an ultra-modern, self-determining strategic weapon. This line of argument can be followed in works such as H.R. Allen's *The Legacy of Lord Trenchard,* David Edgerton's *England and the Aeroplane,* Robin Neillands' *The Bomber War,* Max Hastings' *Bomber Command* and Malcolm Smith's *British Air Strategy Between the Wars.* Stephen Bungay's masterly *The Most Dangerous Enemy* incorporates this line of thinking into what is surely the best history of the Battle of Britain to date. If library space for Battle of Britain literature is limited then this and Geoffrey Wellum's extraordinary personal memoir, *First Light,* will more than suffice. David French's *Raising Churchill's Army* is an excellent source for understanding the Army's failure to get to grips with the RAF's independence.

Considerations of space meant I was unable to go into detail on the problems of strategy, tactics and technology at the outset of the war. These are covered by Alfred Price in *World War Two Fighter Conflict* and Mike Spick in *Pilot Tactics: The Techniques of Daylight Air Combat.* Best of all, however, comes from a pilot who was actually there: Johnnie Johnson's *Wing Leader* and *The Story of Air Fighting* explain the problems and their solutions with admirable clarity and wit. Johnson's is also the finest exposition and critique of the 'Big Wing' controversy, and may be considered to have settled the matter once and for all.

Further Watching

A number of films have been produced, both during and after the Second World War, which add a visual dimension to our understanding of the events described in this book. *The Way to the Stars*, scripted by Terence Rattigan, is the best representation of the civilian relationship with the bombers' war and emphasises the importance of sound in the everyday life of those who lived with the men and machines of the strategic air offensive. *One of Our Aircraft is Missing* shows the closeness of a bomber crew as they try to get home through occupied Holland following the destruction of their aircraft. *The Captured Heart* is a truly remarkable film about Allied PoWs in Germany. Michael Redgrave plays a Czech agent who takes on the identity of a dead British Army officer and is protected by his fellow prisoners from the Gestapo. Accurately researched, the film is at pains to show the daily boredom of life behind the barbed wire, including how a blinded soldier is retrained in Braille using Red Cross-provided tools. Leslie Howard's *The Lamp Still Burns* tells the story of trainee nurses at a busy wartime hospital. Their busy daily lives are detailed, and the operation scenes are accurate and engrossing, as is the moment when a nurse has to remain with a patient who cannot be moved to the shelter during a heavy air raid. Produced at the end of the war, Powell and Pressburger's masterpiece, *A Matter of Life and Death*, is perhaps the greatest British film made at this time. The opening sequence, when David Niven struggles to save his burning bomber aircraft is as accurate a portrayal of a dying aircraft as any, and the scenes set in heaven, with its full complement of bomber crewmen, are both funny and moving. *The Battle of Britain*, made some 20 years after the events it portrays, is still an extraordinarily exciting and accurate representation, and in 2003 was re-released with its original William Walton soundtrack. At one point so many aircraft were assembled by the production team that it represented the 16th largest air force in the world. The film is at pains to show the variety of men who became fighter pilots, away from their elitist image. Most importantly of all it features Bill Foxley in the role of the burned squadron leader, and a scene where Christopher Plummer's damaged fighter inflicts on him the dreaded airman's burn. In 2000, a French production of Marc Dugain's prize-winning novel, *The Officers' Ward*, told the story of an officer with facial injuries inflicted in the First World War, and of his subsequent treatment at the Val du Grace hospital in Paris by one of the founding fathers of plastic surgery. Harold Gillies visited Val du Grace and took back what he learned there to Britain. This often beautiful and moving film conveys the dedication of the surgeons and nursing staff to their patients but is also frank about how they are effectively hidden from the rest of wartime society and their rejection when they try to re-enter it. Most recently, the ITV series *Foyle's War* is a brilliant recreation of life on the Home Front, from police stations to airfields to hospital wards.

Notes

Introduction

1. De Seversky, *Victory through Air Power*, p. 67.
2. 'What is a Lancaster?' cited in Edgerton, *England and the Aeroplane*, plate 14.
3. Harris, *Bomber Offensive*, p. 74.

Chapter One

1. 'Flight Commander', *Cavalry of the Air*, pp. 61–3.
2. See Clark, *Aces High*, p. 75.
3. Smith, *Mick Mannock, Fighter Pilot*, p. 113.
4. Clark, *Aces High*, p. 74.
5. 'Death of an Air Ace, 1918'; Eyewitness – history through the eyes of those who lived it, <www.ibis.com> (1997).
6. 'Cranwell, 1985 AD', *Royal Air Force Quarterly*, Vol. 6, 1935, pp. 436–9.
7. Douglas, *Years of Command*, p. 39.
8. See the Interim Report of the Bureau Enquetes-Accidents issued 25 July 2001 and 'Concorde la Resurrection', in *Paris Match*, 14 December 2001, pp. 32–7.
9. PRO: AIR2/49: Non-leaking Petrol tank, document A.B. 275/757.
10. PRO: AIR2/52: See letter to Air Board Technical Department. For insurance discount, see Lucas, *Silken Canopy*, p. 79.
11. PRO: AIR10/539: See Technical Department Instruction No. 516, 29 February 1918.

12. PRO: AIR40/2044: Visit to the Messerschmitt Works. J. Buchanan minute on Brian Shenstone's report, 6 July 1938, Doc. 228.
13. PRO: AIR40/2044: p. 2.
14. PRO: AVIA10/33: Appendices pp. 14 and 15, RAE Report.
15. PRO: AVIA15/153: Production arrangements for Safety Tanks.
16. PRO:AVIA 15/153: Meeting of 13 November 1939, pp. 4–5, paras. 22 and 23.
17. See PRO: AVIA10/33: Payne to Freeman, 19 December 1939.
18. PRO: AVIA10/33: Protected Tanks – Summary of Action in Hand, by Group Captain Mansell, 27 December 1939.
19. PRO: AIR2/7771: The Dowding Despatch, Appendix, 'Note on the defensive and offensive equipment of our aircraft', para. 3.
20. The Dowding Despatch, para. 4.
21. PRO: AIR40/2113: Captured German tanks.
22. PRO: AIR40/2113: Captured German Tanks, Doc. 142, 'Report of the testing of a rubber petrol tank for aircraft submitted by the Koolhaven works.'
23. PRO: AIR40/213: Reports from November 1940.
24. Douglas Jackson, 'Preface', in Cason, *Treatment of Burns*, p. viii.
25. Rylah, *Critical Care of the Burned Patient*, p. 1.

Chapter Two

1. See Wynn, *Men of the Battle of Britain*.
2. Geoffrey Page, *Shot Down in Flames*, pp. 75–7.
3. Roy Lane, 'Combat!', *The Guinea Pig*, July 1946. The article was published posthumously as Lane had been killed in action in Burma.
4. Gleave, *I had a Row with a German*, pp. 70–1.
5. Maurice Moundsen, cited in Ross, *Richard Hillary*, p. 190.
6. Hillary, *The Last Enemy*, pp. 5–8.
7. 'Playing with Fire', *The Guinea Pig*, July 1978, pp. 20–2.
8. Pat Wells, 'How I became a Guinea Pig', *The Guinea Pig*.
9. James Partridge is the founder and director of the charity Changing Faces which supports and represents children, young people and adults who have disfigurements to the face, hands, and body from any cause. See <www.changingfaces.co.uk>.
10. PRO: AIR20/6452: Plastic Surgery Within the RAF, pp. 1–2.
11. McIndoe, 'Total Reconstruction of the Burned Face', p. 6.

12. Mellor, *Casualties and Medical Statistics*, Table 3b 'RAF Nosological Table for Home Force, 1939–1945, pp. 555–8.
13. PRO: AIR2/7771: Dowding Despatch, p. 8, para. 41.
14. Overy, *The Battle*, p. 86.
15. PRO: AIR2/7771: Dowding Despatch, p. 14, para. 110.
16. Galland, *The First and the Last*, p. 36.
17. PRO: AVIA 6/6703: RAE tests on Linatex. Report by W.D. Douglas.
18. PRO: AIR10/2332: Manual appendix issued May 1940.
19. PRO: AIR10/2332: Protected Fuel Tanks for Aircraft, preliminary to RAF mechanics' manual, issued May 1940.
20. PRO: AIR2/7771: Dowding Despatch, Appendix F, 'Note on the defensive and offensive Equipment of aircraft', paras, 5, 6, 7
21. PRO: AIR16/715: Investigations and reports on war experiences of pilots.
22. Neil, *Gun Button to 'Fire'*, p. 92.
23. Bungay, 'Some Thoughts on "Hurricane Burns"'. Note prepared especially for the author, June 2001.
24. PRO: AIR16/715: Investigations and reports on war experiences of pilots, 25 June 1940.
25. PRO: AIR16/715: Investigations and reports, 1 October 1940.
26. PRO: AIR16/715: Investigations and reports, 1 October 1940, Squadron Leader Rees.
27. PRO: AVIA10/33, OR1/1908: Self-sealing petrol tanks, 30 September 1940.

Chapter Three

1. McIndoe, 'Total Reconstruction of the Burned Face', p. 2.
2. Fox, *Slightly Foxed*, p. 80.
3. 'Misuse of Tannic Acid', *The Lancet*, 16 November 1940, p. 627.
4. Simpson, *The Way of Recovery*, p. 131.
5. Page, *Shot Down in Flames*, p. 87.
6. Page, *Shot Down in Flames*, pp. 94–5.
7. McIndoe, 'Total Reconstruction of the Burned Face', p. 14.
8. *The Lancet*, 'Burns', 16 November 1940, p. 622.
9. Walker, M. (ed.) The Medical Services of the RAN and RAAF, (HMSO, 1946) p. 123.
10. *The Lancet*, 23 November 1940, p. 655.

11. Leo Tremblay, e-mail to author, 27 July 2000. Mr Tremblay died on 6 January 2001.

12. For a full history of this type of anaesthetics see Atkinson and Boulton, *History of Anaesthesia*.

13. PRO: FD1/6479: Hospital Officer D.L. MacKenna to all Class A and IB hospitals in the EMS, October 1940.

14. J. Gordon, *The Lancet*, 30 November 1940, p. 699; W.D. Park, *The Lancet*, 23 November 1940, p. 677.

15. PRO: FD1/6478: Clark to Mellanby, 2 October 1940.

16. PRO: FD1/6479: Drury to Ogilvie, 23 December 1940.

17. PRO: FD1/6479: Ogilvie to Drury, 20 December 1940.

18. PRO: FD1/6479: McIndoe to Drury, 3 January 1941.

19. *Hansard*, 27 November 1940, MacDonald to Thurtle.

20. PRO: AIR49/354: Morley Report December 1943, 'Some Observations on First Aid Treatment of Cases of Burns in the RAF', Doc. 218c, p. 3.

21. PRO: FD1/6478: AVM PMO BC to USofS, AM, 2 October 1943, Doc. No. 205A.

22. PRO: FD1/6478: Morley Report, December 1943, p. 3.

23. McIndoe, 'Total Reconstruction of the Burned Face', pp. 1 and 4.

24. PRO: AIR20/9485: Meeting to consider the modern treatment of burns as applicable to the RAF, 18 September 1951, minutes, p. 7, No. 5.

25. PRO: AIR20/9485: Morley report to Joint Service medical-surgical Conference, July 1954, pp. 7-8.

26. The Home Office, *Civil Defence First Aid Manual* (London: HMSO, 1950), p. 155.

27. *Civil Defence First Aid Manual*, p. 158. I am grateful to the European Space Agency Fellow in the History of Science, Matthew Godwin, for providing me with this information relating to post-war civil defence medical provision.

28. PRO: AIR49/354: Morley to Rexford-Welch.

29. J.N. Barron, 'McIndoe the Gentle Giant', *Annals of the Royal College of Surgeons*, 1985, pp. 205–6.

30. PRO: AIR49/354: Morley to Rexford-Welch, 16 November 1945.

31. PRO: AIR8/79: McIndoe to Portal, 25 October 1943, Doc. 5A.

32. PRO: AIR2/6160: McIndoe, 11 July 1941, Doc. No. 27A.

33. McLeave, *McIndoe, Plastic Surgeon*, p. 104.

34. *The Lancet*, 15 May 1943, pp. 605–9.

35. PRO: AIR2/6160: McIndoe to CME, 26 September 1942, Doc. No. 145B.

36. PRO: AIR/20/10269: DGRAFMS minute, 5 January 1944, p. 22.

37. See PRO: FD1/6483.

38. PRO: AIR2/6160: McIndoe to Drury, 11 February 1941.

39. PRO: AIR8/795: Extension of the Queen Victoria Hospital, East Grinstead. Report of Meeting held on 10 October 1943.

40. J.B. Coates and B.N. Carter (eds.), *The Official History of the US Army Medical Department in World War Two: Surgery in World War Two*, Vols. 1 and 2 (Washington: Office of the Surgeon General, 1962), p. 516.

41. McIndoe, 'Total Reconstruction of the Burned Face'.

42. *Ibid.*, p. 3.

43. Tom Gleave, 'Group Captain tells All', *The Guinea Pig*, Vol. 1, p. 3.

44. Archibald McIndoe, 'The Maestro's Message', *The Guinea Pig*, July 1947, pp. 3–4.

45. Tom Gleave, 'Breakfast at 10am or whenever you felt like it', *The Guinea Pig*, Summer 1964.

46. Peter Kydd, 'Slabbing Remembered', *The Guinea Pig*, April 1950, p. 52.

47. Harold Taubman, 'How I became a Guinea Pig', *The Guinea Pig*, Winter 1965, p. 12.

Chapter Four

1. Hastings, *Bomber Command*, p. 153.

2. Franklin Mellor (ed.), *Casualties and Medical Statistics*.

3. *Ibid.*, p. 549.

4. *Ibid.*, p. 551.

5. *Ibid.*, p. 552.

6. *Ibid.*, p. 555.

7. Mellor, McNalty (eds.), *Principal Medical Lessons from the Second World War*, p. 549, HMSO.

8. Franklin Mellor, *Casualty and Medical Statistics*, pp. 555–63.

9. Rexford-Welch (ed.), *Casualty and Medical Statistics of World War Two*, p. 460.

10. PRO: AIR8/795. Portal to Sec of State, 7 January 1944, p. 2.

11. For a full discussion of German defences such as the *Himmelbett* system of radar-guided fighter systems, the Kammhuber Line and

the Tame and Wild Sow fighter tactics, see Hastings, *Bomber Command*, pp. 234–42. For the latest research into the *Nachtjagd* see Hinchcliffe, *The Other Battle*.

12. Campbell, *The Bombing of Nuremberg*, p. 30.
13. *Ibid.*, p. 50.
14. Flight Sergeant James Brown, cited in Middlebrook, *The Berlin Raids*, p. 236.
15. Details of all the Bomber Command VCs can be found in Falconer, *The Bomber Command Handbook*, pp. 168--71.
16. Flight Sergeant Brown, cited in Middlebrook, *The Berlin Raids*, p. 237.
17. Middlebrook, *Bomber Command War Diaries*, p. 505.
18. *Ibid.*, pp. 601–2.
19. Harold Taubman, '21 years on', *The Guinea Pig*, Summer 1964.
20. 'How your editor became a Guinea Pig', *The Guinea Pig*.
21. See Wells, *Courage*, p. 119.
22. *Ibid.*, p. 119.
23. Cited in Middlebrook, *The Berlin Raids*, pp. 66–7.
24. Cited in Middlebrook, *The Peenemünde Raid*, p. 167.
25. Wells, *Courage*, p. 65.
26. PRO: AIR 20/6452: Plastic surgery in the RAF, December 1943.
27. Archibald McIndoe, 'Valiant for Truth', *National and English Review*, March 1943 and *The Guinea Pig*, Summer 1945, p. 6.
28. PRO: FD1/6300: Meeting of the MRC Burns subcommittee, 12 March 1943, Minutes, p. 2, No. 5.
29. Bill Holmes, 'How I became a Guinea Pig', *The Guinea Pig*, July 1983.
30. Higham, *Bases of Air Strategy*, p. 69.
31. John Harding, *The Guinea Pig*, June 1952.
32. Les Syrett, *The Guinea Pig*, July 1980, p. 12.
33. See Derek Martin, *The Web-footed Guinea Pig*, author's copyright, 2000. Copies of this memoir are available from the libraries of the RAF Museum at Hendon, the Imperial War Museum and Imperial College London.
34. 'How I became a Guinea Pig' in *The Guinea Pig*, June 1952.
35. See PRO: AIR2/4461: Fido Policy, Prime Minister's minute, 26 September 1942; also AIR8/781: WSC to Charles Portal, 9 October 1943 and CAS to WSC, 18 March 1944.

Chapter Five

1. See Rexford-Welch, *The RAF Medical Services*, Vol II, 'Burns Centres', p. 307.
2. See EMS memoranda of 3 October 1940 and 25 February 1941 in PRO: MH76/154. Also The Instructions to SMOs from the Director of the RAFMS on 18 November 1940
3. PRO: AIR49/354: Morley to Rexford-Welch.
4. Rexford-Welch, *The Royal Air Force Medical Service*, p. 531.
5. Archibald McIndoe, 'The First Aid Treatment of Burns', *The Lancet*, 27 September 1941.
6. Rexford-Welch (ed.), *Official History of the Second World War – UK Medical Services, Campaigns* (HMSO, 1953), p. 315.
7. Archibald McIndoe, *The Guinea Pig*, April 1948.
8. See 'The Development of the RCAF Medical Branch', *The Official History of the Canadian Medical Services in World War II*, pp. 361–6.
9. 'Freddie, Dunked off Dieppe is Air/Sea Rescued', *The Guinea Pig*, Vol. 1, 1944, pp. 6–7.
10. *The Official History of the Canadian Medical Services*, p. 363.
11. This section is largely drawn from the official history of the Canadian medical services. See pp. 364–6.
12. PRO: AIR20/10269: H.E. Whittingham to Sir Louis Grieg, 14 July 1943, Doc. 16.
13. PRO: MH76/349: Kirkhope to Maude, 3 May 1945, p. 2.
14. *The Official History of The Canadian Medical Services*, p. 366.
15. Leo Tremblay, 'How I became a Guinea Pig', *The Guinea Pig*, June 1955.
16. Middlebrook and Everitt, *Bomber Command War Diaries*, p. 675.
17. Martha Gellhorn (writer) and Joe Dearing (photographer), 'Men Made Over', *Collier's*, 20 May 1944, p. 32.
18. 'A charming romance', *East Grinstead Gazette*, 24 March 1944.
19. See the collected reports of Major H.E. Snyder, Consultant to Surgeon of 5th Army, in Heaton, Coates & McFetridge, *Surgery in World War Two: Activities of Surgical Consultants*.
20. *The Guinea Pig*, June 1955, p. 24.
21. PRO. WO224/30 ICRC Report, No. 232, 6 August 1943, pp. 3–4.
22. PRO: WO224/30 Note of visit by Werner Buchmueller, Doc. 1382.
23. PRO: WO224/30: ICRC report on Stalag IXB, Doc. 1382, note of visit by Werner Buchmueller.

24. PRO: WO224/30: Note of visit by Gunnar Celander.
25. Archibald Wright Thomson to author, 22 October 2001. The thesis is in Glasgow University, no. 785.
26. PRO: WO224/30: Visit of Dr M.S. Meier, 25 January 1945, Doc. No. 1572.
27. *Prisoner of War*, September 1944, p. 3.
28. *Prisoner of War*, July 1945, p. 8.
29. Jack McEvoy, conversation with the author, November 2001.
30. Maurice Butler, *The Guinea Pig*, July 1984, p. 23.
31. Hussey, *Chance Governs All*, chapter 3.
32. PRO: WO224/30 Charters to ICRC, 10 January 1945.
33. W. Wynne Mason 'Prisoner of War', *The Official History of the Second World War, New Zealand* (HMSO, 1956), p. 170.
34. Obituary of Dr Lawrence J. Somers, *The Guinea Pig*, June 2000.
35. D.L. Charters, 'Gunshot Wound of Both Orbits', *The Lancet*, 19 January 1946, p. 93.
36. Author's conversation with Brian Beveridge, Charters' registrar 1962–68.
37. Registrar of the Order of the British Empire, to Charters, 19 October 1948.

Chapter Six

1. Archibald McIndoe, 'The Maestro's Message', *The Guinea Pig*, 1944.
2. Priestley, *An Inspector Calls*.
3. Hastings, *Bomber Command*, p. 124.
4. *Ibid.*, p. 127.
5. *Ibid.*, p. 128.
6. AIR2/5309: PROs and Press Correspondents participation in operational flights, Stansgate's report of 28 January 1943.
7. Kendrick, *Prime Time: The Biography of Ed Murrow*, pp. 260–3.
8. See PRO: T172/1999.
9. The poster is too large to reproduce successfully but is by Edward Osmond and may be viewed in the Art Department of the Public Records Office. The ICI painting was by Frank Wootton and can be seen in *The Studio* fine arts magazine, Vol. 123, Jan–June 1942, p. 68.
10. PRO: T172/1999: Sir Kingsley Wood, Speech to the Mansion House during the London Wings for Victory Campaign, 5 March 1945.

11. John Hayward, 'Prose Literature since 1939', *Since 1939*, pp. 187–8.

12. Noel Coward, 'Lie in the dark and listen', reproduced by special permission of the author, *The Guinea Pig*, September 1966. From Noel Coward, *Collected Verse*, (London: Methuen 1984) p. 137.

13. Darlow and Hodson, *Terence Rattigan The Man and his Work*, pp. 107–22.

14. McConville, *Immortal*, May 2003.

15. *Ibid.*, p. 41.

16. Helmore, *Air Commentary*, p. 2.

17. Lord Willoughby de Broke to Eric Kennington, 22 September 1942, Archive of the Imperial War Museum.

18. McIndoe, 'Total Reconstruction of the Burned Face', p. 1.

19. McIndoe, 'Valiant for Truth', p. 1.

20. *McIndoe's Army*, Thames Television Productions, 1978.

21. Stella Clapton, *The Guinea Pig Club*, Infinity Films, 2002.

22. Simpson, *The Way of Recovery*, p. 65

23. *Ibid.*, p. 64.

24. 'Bill the Gardner', *The Guinea Pig*, Vol. 1, April 1944, p. 12.

25. 'A charming romance', *East Grinstead Gazette*, 24 March 1944.

26. Simpson, *The Way of Recovery*, p. 64.

27. Betty Bubb, letter to author, 17 July 2003.

28. PRO: AIR20/6452: Plastic Surgery Within the RAF, 'A Survey of the Organisation of a Plastic Surgery Centre Combined with a Burn Treatment Centre' Wing Commander George Morley, 1948 (Air Ministry Publications).

29. Simpson, *The Way of Recovery*, p. 64.

30. *East Grinstead Gazette*, 26 August 1944.

31. 'Report on the AGM of the EGCH', *East Grinstead Gazette*, 9 August 1941, p. 3.

32. *East Grinstead Gazette*, 23 August 1941, 1 August 1942.

33. *East Grinstead Gazette*, 4 July 1942.

34. *East Grinstead Gazette*, 1 August 1942.

35. *East Grinstead Gazette*, 23 August 1941.

36. Conversation with EG theatre nurse Nira Hanbury, February 2002.

37. Mosley, *Faces from the Fire*, p. 67.

38. *East Grinstead Gazette*, 3 July 1943.

39. *East Grinstead Gazette*, 1 August 1943.

40. *Reader's Digest*, November 1943, cited in *The Guinea Pig*, January 1983.

41. Don Armstrong, *The Guinea Pig Club*, Infinity Films, 2002.

42. Julian Brunner, 'The contributions of Sir Archibald McIndoe to the surgery of the hand', *Annals of the Royal College of Surgeons*, Vol. 53, 1973, pp. 27–36.

43. McIndoe, 'Total Reconstruction of the Burned Face', p. 26.

44. PRO: AIR2/4073: 23 May 1940.

45. PRO: AIR2/4073: Minute of 11 November 1941.

46. PRO: AIR2/4073: Dudley-Wright's minute of 21 November 1941.

47. PRO: AIR2/4073: A.1083, 26 December 1941.

48. PRO: AIR2/4073: Minute note, 11 November 1941.

49. Bill Simpson, *The Guinea Pig* Club, Thames TV, 1981.

50. Simpson, *The Way of Recovery*, pp. 64 and 134.

51. PRO: AIR2/6160: Minutes of meeting to discuss Disabled Personnel, Entitlements to Emoluments and Procedure for Invaliding (AC54, 44) 7 November 1944, Section 1A, para. 7(iv).

52. PRO: AIR2/6160: Meeting of the Air Council, 5 December 1944, minutes section e (ii), p. iv.

53. PRO: AIR2/6160: Meeting of 7 November 1944, para. 7(iv).

54. PRO: AIR2/6160: Note by the Under-Secretary of State for Air, 1 March 1945, Doc. 50B, p. 10, para. (c).

55. Wing Commander George Morley, Inaugural McIndoe Lecture, 7 December 1962, 'A tribute to the services of Sir Archibald McIndoe to plastic surgery', *Annals of the Royal College of Surgeons*, p. 404.

56. PRO: AIR2/6160: Special treatment of burns in the RAF. Group Captain D. McLaren to Group Captain Burton, 15 June 1941, Doc. No. 24A.

57. PRO: AIR2/6160: Under-Secretary of State for Air, Note of 1 March 1945.

58. PRO: AIR2/6317: Richards to Humpreyes-Davies, 30 August 1942, Doc. No. 109A.

59. PRO: AIR2/6160: Group Captain D. McLaren to Group Captain Burton, 15 June 1941, para. 4, Doc. 24A.

60. PRO: AIR2/6317: McIndoe to Philip Babington, 18 May 1942, Doc. 43A, p. 1.

61. Obituary of Robert Wright, *The Guinea Pig*, January 1991.

62. Sir Hugh Dowding to Chief Guinea Pig Tom Gleave, *The Guinea Pig*, Christmas 1967.

63. PRO: AIR2/6317: Mackay to Kirk, 30 April 1943, Doc. 101A.

64. PRO: AIR2/6317: Richards to Humphreyes-Davies, 30 August 1943, Doc. 109A, para. 3.

65. PRO: AIR2/6317: Mackay to Kirk Ref no. E23316, cited in Sandford to Humphreyes-Davies, 24 August 1943, Doc. 149A.

66. PRO: AIR2/6317: Sandford to Humphreyes-Davies, 24 August 1944, Doc. 149A.

67. PRO: AIR2/6160: Disabled Personnel – Entitlements to Emoluments and Procedure for Invaliding, November 1949, Doc. 1A, Minutes.

68. PRO: AIR8/795: Portal to McIndoe, 3 November 1944.

69. PRO: AIR2/6010: Curtis to Kirk, 10 April 1947, Doc. 136A.

70. PRO: AIR2/6317: Babington to McIndoe, 10 November 1941, Doc. 8A.

71. Bernard Arch, *The Guinea Pig*, January 1973.

72. First London performance of *Lady in the Dark*, 31 May 1944. *The Guinea Pig*, January 1973, p. 15.

73. McIndoe, 'Valiant for Truth', *National and English Review*, cited in *The Guinea Pig*, January 2000.

74. Cyril Connolly, 'Comment', *Horizon*, April 1943, Volume VII, Number 40, p. 220.

75. John Hayward, *Since 1939*, pp. 188–9.

76. McIndoe, 'An Open Letter from the Maestro', *The Guinea Pig*, Volume 1, p. 2.

77. Martha Gellhorn, 'Men Made Over', *Collier's*, 20 May 1944, pp. 32–5.

78. BBC Christmas broadcast, 25 December 1945, transcribed in *East Grinstead Gazette*, 29 December.

Chapter Seven

1. McIndoe, 'Total Reconstruction of the Burned Face', p. 26.

2. Connelly, *Reaching for the Stars*, p. 134.

3. *The Guinea Pig*, January 1993, p. 4.

4. See Edgerton, *England and the Aeroplane*.

5. *Time*, 27 September 1948.

6. McIndoe, 'Valiant For Truth: The Maestro's Message', *The Guinea Pig*, April 1953, pp. 1–3.

7. Verrier, *The Bomber Offensive*, pp. 5 and 98.

8. Henry Standen, *The Guinea Pig*, August 1948, pp. 33–5.

9. *The Battle of Britain*, 1967, prod. Salzman and Fisz.

10. Cited in Tony Aldgate, 'The Battle of Britain on Film', in Crang and Addison, *The Burning Blue*, p. 215.
11. *The Guinea Pig Club*, Infinity Films, 2001.
12. *The Guinea Pig*, August 1948, p. 7.
13. *Time*, 27 September 1948, p. 26.
14. Ava Gardner, *My Story* (London: Bantam Press, 1990), pp. 233–5.
15. *The Guinea Pig*, Christmas 1958.
16. 'Aims and Objects', *The Guinea Pig*, April 1944, p. 5.
17. *The Guinea Pig*, July 1957, p. 23.
18. Author's correspondence with Toper, 31 January 2002.
19. Author's conversation with Allaway, 22 February 2002.
20. *The Guinea Pig*, July 1982, p. 34.
21. *The Guinea Pig*, New Year 1983, p. 22.
22. See <www.limblessassociation.org>.

Conclusions

1. Allan D. English, 'A Predisposition to Cowardice? Aviation Psychology and the Genesis of Lack of Moral Fibre', *War and Society*, 1995, 13: 15–34, p. 15.
2. Mazower, *Dark Continent*, p. 1.
3. See Edgerton, *England and the Aeroplane*.
4. Sebald, *On the Natural History of Destruction*, p. 17.
5. See Hastings, *Bomber Command*; Neillands, *The Bomber War*.
6. See Calder, *The Myth of the Blitz* and *The People's War*; Marwick, *The Home Front*; Smith, *Britain and 1940, History, Myth and Popular Memory*.
7. Edgerton, *England and the Aeroplane*, p. 107. See also the collected works of Sebastian Ritchie.
8. See Jeremy Crang, 'The British Soldier on the Home Front' in Calder and Addison, *A Time to Kill*.

Bibliography

Primary Sources

This is the first time the official files held at the Public Records Office at Kew on the work of Archibald McIndoe at East Grinstead have ever been accessed by a biographer or historian. All the PRO files used for this book are as follows:

AIR10/2332	Preliminary note to RAF mechanics manual: 'Protected Fuel tanks for Aircraft'
AIR10/539	Self-sealing fuel tanks in two seater aeroplanes
AIR2/11909	Air Ministry Contracts
AIR2/4073	Authority for personnel invalided from RAF to wear uniform whilst under treatment
AIR2/4461	Fog Installation and Dispersal Organisation, policy (FIDO)
AIR2/49	Non-leaking petrol tanks by Lanser
AIR2/52	Self-sealing fuel tanks
AIR2/5309	Press participation in operational flights
AIR2/6160	Disabled Personnel – Entitlements to Emoluments and Procedure for Invaliding
AIR2/6317	Facially disfigured personnel – scheme for employment during convalescence
AIR2/7771	Dowding Despatch on the Battle of Britain
AIR20/11796	FIDO
AIR20/10269	Plastic Surgery in the RAF (II)

AIR20/3123	FIDO
AIR20/4677	FIDO
AIR20/6452	Plastic Surgery within the RAF
AIR20/9485	Meeting to consider the modern treatment of burns as applicable to the RAF
AIR40/2044	Visit to the Messerschmitt works
AIR40/2113	German aircraft and fuel tanks; reports on captured aircraft
AIR49/354	Burns and plastic surgery
AIR49/354	First Aid Treatment of Burns in the RAF
AIR6/715	Investigations and reports on war experiences of pilots
AIR8/781	FIDO
AIR8/795	Queen Victoria Hospital Extension
AIR2/982-5	Messrs Calthrop Aerial Patents Ltd, proposals regarding parachutes
AVIA10/33	Self-sealing petrol tanks, development and production, 1939-40
AVIA15/1000	Design Branch specifications, Lancaster I/P1
AVIA15/153	Production arrangements for safety petrol tanks
AVIA15/2979	Goodyear tanks for British aircraft, investigations of
AVIA15/3190	Rubber for self-sealing tanks
AVIA15/590	Specification of differences: Manchester/Lancaster aircraft with Merlin engines
AVIA18/705	Conclusions of report on captured Messerschmitt 109
AVIA6/3450	Dropping tests of inner bag type of fuel tank
AVIA6/5184	Dropping of petrol tanks to investigate and overcome causes of fire
AVIA6/6703	RAE tests on Linatex
AVIA6/8663	Ammunition tests against self-sealing tanks
AVIA6/8905	Self-sealing covers on fuel tanks
FD1/6300	Medical Research Council, sub-committee on burns
FD1/6301	Burns sub-committee
FD1/6366	Burns sub-committee
FD1/6478	Treatment of burns
FD1/6479	Treatment of burns
MH76/349	Queen Victoria Hospital extension

MH76/154   Treatment of burns
T172/1999   'Wings for Victory' campaign, speeches
WO222/19   Medical Research Council: sub-committee on burns
WO224/30   Report on Stalag IXB

Official Histories

The Official Medical History of the Second World War, edited by S. Rexford-Welch (HMSO, 1952–1972) includes the following volumes used here:

Dunn, P., (ed.) The Emergency Medical Service. HMSO, 1952.

Franklin Mellor, W., (ed.), Casualties and Medical Statistics. HMSO, 1972.

MacNalty, S., and Franklin-Mellor, W., (eds.), The Principal Lessons of the Second World War. HMSO, 1968.

Rexford-Welch, S., (ed.), The Royal Air Force Medical Service. HMSO, 1954.

Coates, J.B., and Carter, B.N., (eds.), The Official History of the US Army Medical Department in World War Two: Surgery in World War Two. Washington, DC: Office of the Surgeon General, 1962.

Coates, B., and McFetridge, E., (eds.), Blood Programme in World War Two. Historical Unit of the US Army Medical Service, 1964.

Coates, B.; Heaton, C.; and McFetridge, E., (eds.), Surgery in World War Two: Activities of the Surgical Consultants. Historical Unit of the US Army Medical Service, 1962.

Collier, B., The Defence of the United Kingdom. HMSO, 1957.

Walker, M., (ed.), Medical Services of the RAN and RAAF. HMSO, 1946.

Webster, C., and Frankland, N., The Strategic Air Offensive against Germany. HMSO, 1961.

Official History of The Canadian Medical Services, 'Development of the RCAF Medical Branch', Vol. 2 1939–1945, Ottawa Queen's Printer, 1953.

Wynne-Mason, W. Official History of New Zealand in the Second World War, War History Branch, Department of Internal Affairs.

Newspapers and periodicals

The Guinea Pig
Royal Air Force Quarterly
Journal of the RAF Staff College

East Grinstead Observer
Prisoner of War
Journal of Burn Care and Rehabilitation
The Lancet
The Studio
Horizon
Annals of the Royal College of Surgeons

Secondary and other sources

Air Ministry Productions, *Bomber Command*. London: HMSO, 1941.

Alexander, D.A., 'Burn victims after a major disaster: reactions of patients and their care-givers', *Journal of Burns Care and Rehabilitation*, Vol. 19, 1993.

Allen, H.R., *The Legacy of Lord Trenchard*. London: Cassell, 1972.

Atkinson, R.S., and Boulton, *A History of Anaesthesia*. London: Parthenon, 1989.

Bennett, J., 'A History of East Grinstead Hospital', *Journal of the British Association of Plastic Surgery*, 1988 (pamphlet issued separately).

Bishop, E., *Hurricane*. Shrewsbury: Airlife Publishing, 1986.

Bishop, E., *McIndoe's Army*. London: Grub Street, 2001.

Black, Jonathan, *The Graphic Art of Eric Kennington*. London: UCL Publications, 2000.

Borrie, J., *Despite Captivity*. London: Kimber, 1975.

British Council, *Since 1939*, Volumes 1 and 2, London: Reader's Union, 1948.

Brunner, J., 'The Contributions of Sir Archibald McIndoe to the Surgery of the Hand', *Annals of the Royal College of Surgeons*, 1973.

Bungay S., *Alamein*. London: Aurum, 2002.

Bungay, S., 'Some Thoughts on "Hurricane Burns"' London, June 2001.

Bungay, S., *The Most Dangerous Enemy*. London: Aurum, 2000.

Burleigh, M., *The Third Reich, A New History*. London: Macmillan, 2000.

Calder, A., 'The Battle of Britain and Pilots' Memoirs', in Addison and Crang, (eds.), *The Burning Blue*. London: Pimlico, 2000.

Calder, A. *The Myth of the Blitz*. London: Jonathan Cape, 1991.

Calder, A., *The People's War*. London: Granada, 1965.

Calder, A., and Addison, P., (eds.), *A Time to Kill*. London: Pimlico, 1997.

Campbell, J., *The Bombing of Nuremberg*. London: Allison & Busby, 1973.

Capka, J., *Red Sky at Night*. London: Blond, 1958.

Cason, J.S., *Treatment of Burns*. London: Chapman and Hall, 1981.

Charlton, L., *The Air Defence of Great Britain*. London: Penguin, 1938.

Clark, A., *Aces High!* London: Weidenfeld & Nicolson, 1973.

Connelly, Mark, *Reaching for the Stars, a New History of Bomber Command*. London: I.B. Tauris, 2001.

Crang, J.A. and Addison, P., (eds.) *The Burning Blue*. London: Pimlico, 2000.

Darlow, M., and Hodson, T., *Terence Rattigan, the Man and his Work*. London: Quartet Books, 1982.

Dennison, A., *A Cottage Hospital Grows Up: The Story of The Queen Victoria Hospital, East Grinstead*. London: Anthony Blond, 1963.

De Seversky, A., *Victory through Air Power*. London: Hutchinson, 1942.

Douglas, S., *Years of Command*. London: Macmillan, 1963.

Downie, P., (ed.), *Cash's Textbook of General, Medical and Surgical Conditions for Physiotherapists*. London: Faber and Faber, 1990.

Edgerton, D., *England and the Aeroplane*. London: Macmillan, 1990.

Falconer, J., *The Bomber Command Handbook*. Stroud: Sutton, 1998.

Faulks, S., *The Fatal Englishman*. London: Hutchinson, 1996.

Ferris, J., 'Fighter Defence before Fighter Command', *Journal of Military History*, Volume 3, October 1999.

'Flight Commander' (Helmore), *Cavalry of the Air*. London: E.J. Burrow & Co, 1918.

Formanek, V., *Stories of Brave Guinea Pigs*. Hailsham: J & KH Publishing, 1998.

Fox, Angela, *Slightly Foxed*. London: Collins, 1986.

Galland, A., *The First and The Last: The German Fighter Force in World War II*. London: Methuen, 1955.

Gleave, T., *I had a Row with a German*. London: Macmillan, 1941.

Harris, A., *Bomber Offensive*. London: Collins, 1947.

Harrisson, T., 'War Books', *Horizon*, 1941.

Hastings, M., *Bomber Command*. London: Michael Joseph, 1979.

Helmore, *Air Commentary*. London: Allen & Unwin, 1942.

Hewison, R., *Under Siege: Literary Life in London, 1939–1945*. London: Methuen, 1977.

Higham, R., *Bases of Air Strategy*. Shrewsbury: Airlife Publications, 1998.

Hillary, R., *The Last Enemy*. London: Macmillan, 1942.

Hinchcliffe, P., *The Other Battle*. Shrewsbury: Airlife, 2001.

Hodgkinson, C., *Best Foot Forward*. London: Odhams Press, 1957.

Holmes, H., *Avro Lancaster, The Definitive Record*. Shrewsbury: Airlife, 2001.

Hough, R., and Richards, D., *The Battle of Britain: The Jubilee History*. London: Hodder & Stoughton, 1989.

Howard J., 'Prose Literature since 1939', *Since 1939*. London: The British Council, 1946.

Hussey, M., *Chance Governs All*. London: Macmillan, 2001.

Jackson, D., 'Preface', in Cason, J., *Treatment of Burns*. London: Chapman & Hall, 1981.

Jackson, D., 'The Evolution of Burn Treatment', *Journal of Burn Care and Rehabilitation*, Volume 32, 1991.

Janeway, C., 'Plasma, the Transport Fluid for Blood Cells and Humors', in Wintrobe, M., *Blood, Pure and Eloquent*. New York: McGraw Hill, 1980.

Johnson, J.E., *The Story of Air Fighting*. London: Hutchinson, 1964.

Johnson, J.E., *Wing Leader*. London: Chatto and Windus, 1956.

Kendrick, A., *Prime Time: The Biography of Ed Murrow*. Boston: Little, Brown, 1969.

Kennington, E., *Drawing the RAF*. Oxford: Oxford University Press, 1942.

Kater, M.H., *Doctors Under Hitler*. Chapel Hill: University of North Carolina Press, 1989.

Koestler, A., 'The Birth of A Myth', *Horizon*, 1943.

Le Souef, L., *To War Without a Gun*. Perth: Artlook, 1980.

Low, A.M., *Parachutes in Peace and War*. London: John Gifford, 1942,

Lucas, J., *The Silken Canopy*. Shrewsbury: Airlife, 1997.

Maclean, C., *The Heavens are Not Too High*. London: William Kimber, 1957.

McIndoe, A., 'Total Reconstruction of the Burned Face.' Bradshaw Lecture of 1958, *Library of the Royal College of Surgeons*.

McIndoe, A., 'First Aid Treatment of Burns', *The Lancet*, 1941.

McLeave, H., *McIndoe, Plastic Surgeon*. London: Frederick Muller, 1961.

Marwick, A., *The Home Front*. London: Macmillan, 1976.

Mazower, M., *Dark Continent*. London: Penguin, 1998.

Meilinger, P., 'The Historiography of Air Power, Theory and Decline', *Journal of Military History*, April 2000.

Middlebrook, M., and Everitt, K., (eds.), *The Bomber Command War Diaries*. London: Viking, 1985.

Middlebrook, M., *The Battle of Hamburg*. London: Allen Lane, 1980.

Middlebrook, M., *The Berlin Raids*. London: Viking, 1988.

Middlebrook, M., *The Peenemünde Raid*. London: Allen Lane, 1982.

Moore, B., and Fedorowich, K., *Prisoners-of-War and Their Captors in World War II*. Oxford: Berg, 1996.

Morgan and Shacklady, *Spitfire: the History*. London: Key Publications, 1987.

Mosley, L., *Faces from the Fire*. London: Weidenfeld and Nicolson, 1962.

Mowlem, R., 'Foreword' in Muir, Barclay, Settle, *Burns and their Treatment*. London: Butterworths, 1987.

Neil, Tom, *Gun Button to 'Fire'*. London: William Kimber, 1987.

Neillands, R., *The Bomber War*. London: John Murray, 2001.

Nichol, J., and Rennell, T., *The Last Escape*. London: Viking, 2002.

Overy, R., *The Battle*. London: Penguin, 2000.

Page, A.G., *Shot Down in Flames*. London: Grub Street, 1999; originally published as *Tale of a Guinea Pig*, Canterbury: Wingham Press, 1991.

Pape, R., *Boldness Be My Friend*. London: Elek Books, 1953.

Partridge, James, *Changing Faces*. London: Thames and Hudson, 1990.

Penn, J., *The Right to Look Human*. Johannesburg: McGraw Hill, 1965.

Pound, Reginald, *Gillies, Surgeon Extraordinary*. London: Michael Joseph, 1964.

Price, A., *World War Two Fighter Conflict*. London: Macdonald & Jane's, 1975.

Priestley, J.B., *An Inspector Calls*. London: Faber & Faber, 1945.

Probert, H., *Bomber Harris: His Life and Times*. London: Greenhill, 2001.

Proctor, R., *Hitler's Luftwaffe in the Spanish Civil War*. Connecticut: Greenwood Press, 1983.

RAF Museum Series: The Lancaster Manual. London: Greenhill, 2003.

Rank, B.K., *Heads and Hands*. London: Gower Medical Publishing, 1987.

Rattigan, T., *The Flare Path*. London: Hamish Hamilton, 1942.

Rawnsley, C.F., and Wright, R., *Night Fighter*. London: Collins, 1957.

Rhys, J., *England is my Village*. London: Faber & Faber, 1940.

Rickenbacker, E., *Fighting the Flying Circus*. New York: Stokes, 1919.

Ritchie, S., *Industry and Air Power*. London: Frank Cass, 1997.

Rolf, D., *Prisoners of the Reich*. London: Leo Cooper, 1998.

Ross, D., *Richard Hillary*. London: Grub Street, 2000.

Rylah, C. (ed.), *Critical Care of the Burned Patient*. Cambridge: Cambridge University Press, 1992.

Sebald, W.G., *On the Natural History of Destruction*. London: Hamish Hamilton, 2003.

Simpson, W., *One of Our Pilots is Safe*. London: Hamish Hamilton, 1942.

Simpson, W., *The Way of Recovery*. London: Hamish Hamilton, 1944.

Smith, Adrian, *Mick Mannock, Fighter Pilot: Myth, Life and Politics*, London: Palgrave, 2001.

Smith, M., *Britain and 1940: History, Myth and Popular Memory*. London: Routledge, 2002.

Smith, Malcolm, *British Air Strategy Between the Wars*. Oxford: Oxford University Press, 1984.

Spick, M., *Fighter Pilot Tactics: the Techniques of Daylight Air Combat*. Cambridge: Patrick Stephens, 1983.

Steel, N., and Hall, P., *Tumult in the Clouds*. London: Hodder & Stoughton, 1997.

Terraine, J., *The Right of the Line*. London: Hodder & Stoughton, 1985.

Underhill, E., *et al.*, 'Blood Concentration', *Archives of Internal Medicine*, 1921.

Verrier, A., *The Bomber Offensive*. London: Batsford, 1968.

Wells, M., *Courage and Air Warfare*. London: Frank Cass, 1995.

Williams, P., and Harrison, T., *McIndoe's Army*. London: Pelham Books, 1979.

Wright, R., *Dowding and the Battle of Britain*. London: Macdonald, 1969.

Wynn, K.G., (ed.), *Men of the Battle of Britain*. London: Gliddon Books, 1989.

Index